WALKING IN C

21 Shorter Walks

HEATHER MACDERMID

Photographs by Greg Lucas

CORDEE – LEICESTER

ISBN 1 871890 18 7

British Library Cataloguing in Publication Data
A catalogue record for this book is available from the British Library

We hope this guide will enable and encourage people to enjoy walking the footpaths of Charnwood Forest. Although every effort has been made to keep the guide as clear and accurate as possible, we are sorry that we cannot take any responsibility for your walks, so please take care.

All trade enquiries to:
CORDEE, 3a De Montfort Street, Leicester LE1 7HD

Cover photograph taken in Bradgate Park by Greg Lucas

Maps by Jeff Nightingale

CONTENTS

The famous 'Bomb Rocks'. At 650 million years old, they are some of the oldest in Britain.

INTRODUCTION

'Walkers should exert themselves enough to become slightly breathless but not so much as to interfere with conversation.'
Dr William Bird . . . Sonning Common Health Centre leaflet, 1996

Ten years ago when producing **Walks around Charnwood** I thought of 8–10 miles as a short walk. A decade later, that book is out of print and I, being nearer my own sell-by date, have come to realise that 4–6 miles is a more reasonable estimate of a good short walk for most people. The walks in this book are all under 6 miles, many with possible short cuts and stopping points on the way.

You don't have to do a long walk at high speed to keep you fit. A short walk undertaken for pleasure makes perfectly healthy exercise. Each walk in this book offers you two or three hours in beautiful countryside with the added value of knowledge that this is doing you good!

They should be an ideal choice for family groups, for couples wishing to explore the countryside and its past secrets, for solo walkers wanting quiet relaxation, for birdwatchers, nature lovers and strollers wanting to photograph, to pause to look, to talk, eat or drink and return refreshed.

But as a compromise for my many friends who still want a longer stretch for their legs, the walks in the book are arranged so that they can be joined together to make a satisfying long day out.

The introductions to each walk give details of how to get to starting places from villages or recognised country parks. The walks are all circular and can be started at various points.

Transport. Almost all these places are accessible by bus, though bus users may need to walk an extra mile or so for bus stops in the heart of Charnwood. Bus Line (0116 251 1411) give helpful information. Bus maps and timetables are available from Midland Fox offices in Charles Street (6 Hannam Court) LE1 3FS and from County Hall, Glenfield.

Car parks: There are car parks at most of the starting points, but if you do have to park at the roadside, please do so with care and consideration. Some pubs will allow parking in their car parks if you intend to eat or drink there, but do ask permission.

Refreshment: Most of these routes have pubs or cafes where you can eat at the beginning, end or middle of the walk. Where no pubs are available en route you are advised to provide yourself with a picnic.

Equipment; Sensible footwear and suitable clothing and a bag to sling over your shoulder, with waterproofs (to sit on!) and some emergency food and drink is really all you need for these walks. Although some of the terrain is hilly, the paths are well marked, well stiled and well used and you are never very far from habitation.

If you are of a cautious disposition you might like to carry a compass and whistle (I do!) and a First Aid kit (mine contains elastoplast and suncream).

Maps: Most of the walks in this book are on Pathfinder maps SK41/51. A few spill over onto SK40/50. It would be well worth getting these maps, to help you see the whole picture. You can fold them to show the route you are using, and carry them in a clear plastic bag to keep them clean while you are walking!

Items of interest are indicated in the introductions. These are mainly historical and geological because rocks, buildings and famous events stay comparatively unchanged and still. I leave the flora and fauna to your own sharp eyes! There are animals and plants to be seen everywhere, in different places and seasons on these walks. The kestrels, the deer, the bluebells and wild garlic and ragged robin are joys for you to discover for yourself (but notice boards in the various nature reserves and country parks will give you some clues as to what to look out for).

The route descriptions give the mileage and a brief description of the kind of terrain you can expect, with possible short cuts or escape routes. 2 miles an hour is quite a good pace to average in this sort of countryside. Allow yourself longer for lingering!

The instructions for each walk are given as simply as possible, with enough detail to keep you on the right track. The paragraphs are numbered to help you keep your place in the text. Any additional information is usually relegated to the introductions, to be read when you are seated comfortably.

To join walks together you can choose two which start from the same place or, with a little more ingenuity, insert a second from junctions which should be clear from the maps.

If you start at any mid-point in the walk, go back to paragraph 1 when you reach the end of the instructions and continue until you reach your starting point. (The map should make this clear.)

Enjoy your walks!

Heather MacDermid

THE CHARNWOOD STORY

An introductory note to Charnwood:
'The now lofty chains of the Alps, the Pyrennees, the Andes and in fact nearly all the mountain ranges of the world, are but mere children . . . compared with the venerable antiquity of the Leicestershire hill country'.
Dr Horace Brown 1887 (quoted by C N Hadfield, Charnwood Forest p.4)

Charnwood is the area a few miles north west of Leicester in a hilly region of ancient, pre-Cambrian rocks. Most Leicestershire people are surprised to learn that in Charnwood we have some of the oldest rocks known anywhere in England and that a volcano erupted here around High Sharpley, near Whitwick, 700 million years ago. The ash, lava, steam and rocks were thrown out for many miles, into what was then sea. When the volcano ceased, this mud and debris was pressurised, under the water, into rocks and then folded, contorted and tipped.

Millions of years later, in the Ice Age, some of these huge rocks were pushed along and we see many perched precariously in odd places.

Several of our walks follow geological trails where you can pick out the amazing variety of these complex ancient rocks. You can follow the rock trail over the Warren Hills and through the Outwoods and over Beacon Hill and down to Blackbrook reservoir. In Bradgate park you can walk along a line of granite-like bedrock to sharply pointed hills made up of volcanic dust highly compressed into agglomerates and slates near Swithland Woods. We are amazed as we pause at the rocky outcrops in Bradgate and Swithland and Cademan at the force and extent of the volcanic pressures which threw up so much great rock over such a wide area.

From the top of Bardon Hill we can see into the core of the volcanic plug. Near Whitwick and Mt St Bernard's the grand finale is to look down into Peldar Tor quarry where whole chunks of Charnwood rock are being taken out from the accumulated coarse volcanic material to make great motorways. We marvel, as we look down into the great holes in the ground where modern machines, looking like Dinky toys, dig into the heart of the extinct volcano, exposing the layers of rocks laid down hundreds of millions of years ago.

The rocks have been quarried for many centuries. The quarries from former ages have been softened and beautified by time. The old slate quarries in Swithland wood, are now awe-inspiring, steep-sided, tree-edged rocky lakes of blue water but the present quarries are harsh scars, a blight on the landscape in many of these beautiful walks.

Charnwood is surprisingly different from the rest of Leicestershire. The soil is shallow and difficult to farm and the land has never been densely inhabited. Iron Age people made hill forts on the hilltops of Beacon and Buddon and the Romans quarried slate in Swithland. They made tracks into the forest to exploit the rocky woodland. When the Saxons settled here, they used the forest and governed it with forest laws, from swanimote courts. These courts, held in clearings and at distinctive rocky points, must have had well used tracks, from outlying farmsteads, but there were only ever isolated settlements in the forest, and even now the villages in Charnwood are small.

The rocky, wooded land was, however, good for hunting and when the Normans conquered England, William the Conqueror rewarded his knights with land and castles on the edge of the Charnwood forest. In Norman times four manors were established here. The borders of their land met in the 'waste' lands of Charnwood.

Pockets of this 'waste' land were gradually cleared of woodland and settled by small communities of farmers and monks in places like Ulverscroft Abbey which was an early clearing in the forest. Other early enclosures of land in the forest can be detected through the tell tale names of 'haws' and 'hays', an indication that they were cleared, hedged and protected by thorny hedges. We pass near Aldermans Haw, Old Hays and Bondman Hays, all early clearings of the forest waste.

The richer, more favoured landowners and clerics hunted in the forest and gradually established deer parks with high banks and paling to prevent their deer wandering. Deer Parks were established at Bardon, Beaumanor and Bradgate in about 1150 and 1250. We go near many of these parks. Only Bradgate, constructed for the Greys of Groby Castle, still exists as a deer park. The others that we pass, like that at Old Hays, have only the remains of banks and ditches and walls beside the footpath to show us where their boundaries were.

Bardon Deer park, once owned by Alexander Comyn of Whitwick castle, has been quarried beyond recognition but with a bit of detective work we can pick out the walls, banks and ditches of the deer park, and with a great deal of imagination we can stand on the top of the hill where the summer house once stood and see the glories which the royal picnickers so admired when they visited in August 1840.

All our walks take place in this area, a landscape of volcanic rocks and ancient woodland, deer parks and small outlying villages.

Much of the woodland has now gone, but patches remain. We pass woods like Bardon, Birch Hill, and Buddon Woods, which are recorded in documents as far back as 1200 and we go through The Outwoods and Sheet Hedges, mentioned in 1300 and Holly Hayes and Johns Lee Wood which are documented in the 16th century.

Individual trees in Bradgate have been dated (by dendrochronology) back to 1595 and others in the park are thought to be even older. Many of the trees in the park were coppiced or topped out, a process which prolongs the life of a tree. The 'Copped oak' tree at Copt Oak, blown down in the 1855 gale, was reputedly 2000 years old, 20' high and 24' in circumference. This great tree, which stood near the present church, was an important landmark and meeting place long before the church was built.

The tree has gone, but we can still see the great slabs of isolated rocks which were used as meeting places in the forest by our Saxon and Norman ancestors. In walk 20 we pass the Swanimote rock where forest courts were held to pass judgment on forest law-breakers, miscreants who poached the lord's animals or took wood from his trees or failed to fulfil their obligations to provide labour to build or maintain his deer park paling. We pass other spectacular rocks like High Cademan and High Sharpley (near Whitwick) in the same walk.

Many of the tracks that must have been used to reach the swanimote courts are now on private land. The Enclosure Act of 1808, which was designed to make for more efficient farming, parcelled uncultivated moorland into sections for individual landowners, who were required to fence off their boundaries. It also brought new, straight roads (and towered churches) to Charnwood. The better roads eventually made for easier transport which in turn made for an increase in commerce and industrialisation.

For those with a taste for industrial archaeology there is, in some of these walks, the added interest of Victorian transport, canals and railway lines which took the coal from the mines near Whitwick and Swannington. We can now walk along many of the disused lines of rail and dismantled canals and admire the engineering skills and sheer physical effort involved in cutting through this hard rock, building reservoirs, dams and bridges to enable coal and passengers to be hauled on trains up inclines, or by water round hills and valleys. These features now have a distant charm and make interesting items on our walks.

The 20th century motorways which cut such a swathe through the lovely countryside do not have such attractions for our walks. They cut through Charnwood in a heartbreaking and noisy way. The proliferat-

LOCATION MAP

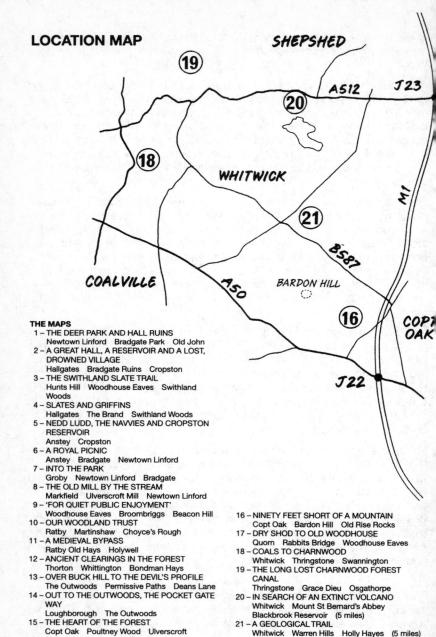

SHEPSHED

A512   J23

19

20

18

WHITWICK

21

M1

COALVILLE

A50

BARDON HILL

16

COP
OAK

J22

THE MAPS

1 – THE DEER PARK AND HALL RUINS
   Newtown Linford   Bradgate Park   Old John
2 – A GREAT HALL, A RESERVOIR AND A LOST,
   DROWNED VILLAGE
   Hallgates   Bradgate Ruins   Cropston
3 – THE SWITHLAND SLATE TRAIL
   Hunts Hill   Woodhouse Eaves   Swithland
   Woods
4 – SLATES AND GRIFFINS
   Hallgates   The Brand   Swithland Woods
5 – NEDD LUDD, THE NAVVIES AND CROPSTON
   RESERVOIR
   Anstey   Cropston
6 – A ROYAL PICNIC
   Anstey   Bradgate   Newtown Linford
7 – INTO THE PARK
   Groby   Newtown Linford   Bradgate
8 – THE OLD MILL BY THE STREAM
   Markfield   Ulverscroft Mill   Newtown Linford
9 – 'FOR QUIET PUBLIC ENJOYMENT'
   Woodhouse Eaves   Broombriggs   Beacon Hill
10 – OUR WOODLAND TRUST
   Ratby   Martinshaw   Choyce's Rough
11 – A MEDIEVAL BYPASS
   Ratby Old Hays   Holywell
12 – ANCIENT CLEARINGS IN THE FOREST
   Thorton   Whittington   Bondman Hays
13 – OVER BUCK HILL TO THE DEVIL'S PROFILE
   The Outwoods   Permissive Paths   Deans Lane
14 – OUT TO THE OUTWOODS, THE POCKET GATE
   WAY
   Loughborough   The Outwoods
15 – THE HEART OF THE FOREST
   Copt Oak   Poultney Wood   Ulverscroft

16 – NINETY FEET SHORT OF A MOUNTAIN
   Copt Oak   Bardon Hill   Old Rise Rocks
17 – DRY SHOD TO OLD WOODHOUSE
   Quorn   Rabbits Bridge   Woodhouse Eaves
18 – COALS TO CHARNWOOD
   Whitwick   Thringstone   Swannington
19 – THE LONG LOST CHARNWOOD FOREST
   CANAL
   Thringstone   Grace Dieu   Osgathorpe
20 – IN SEARCH OF AN EXTINCT VOLCANO
   Whitwick   Mount St Bernard's Abbey
   Blackbrook Reservoir   (5 miles)
21 – A GEOLOGICAL TRAIL
   Whitwick   Warren Hills   Holly Hayes   (5 miles)

10

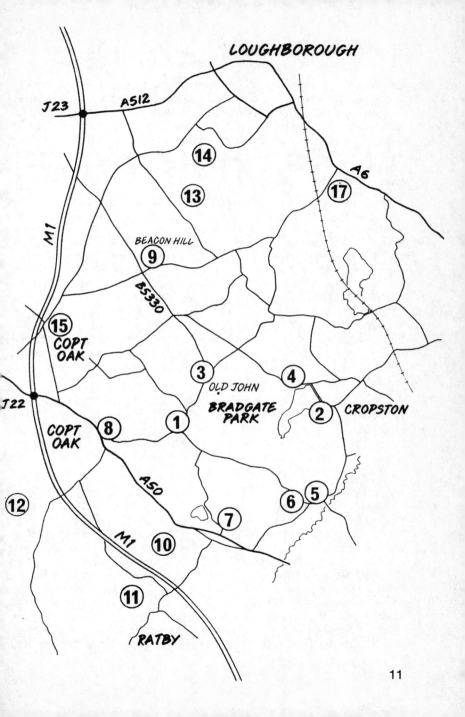

ing distibutor roads impinge on the precious quiet of the countryside and often force us to divert from the ancient lines of footpath.

Several of the routes in this book are in process of being diverted to make way for extensions and changes in quarry workings. Bardon Hill is now being MOVED to a neighbouring site! (Rocks are quarried and soil dumped to make a new hill beside the old one.) Paths are still being altered near Groby quarries, where local hostility to quarry extension has resulted in improved attitudes to environmental concerns and in additional paths for walkers. (We shall welcome the new path to Groby Pool.)

There has been much improvement in public access to Charnwood. Many high places which were once privately owned after the Enclosure Act have now been bought and donated as gifts of open space for the quiet enjoyment of the public. We still cannot walk freely up to Ives Head, an old swanimote meeting place, and access is denied to Charnwood Lodge. The Hangingstone Rocks now have Private signs, although in 1950 it was confidently expected that the golf club had bought the land 'with the intention of giving to members of the public the same degree of access as has been customary in the past, while preserving its amenities and its character as a golf course.' (Guy Paget and Lionel Irvine, The County Books, Leicestershire.) Unfortunately such assurance was misplaced. The present management of the golf course do not acknowledge any commitment to public access.

But the situation elsewhere is much improved since 1926 when J B Firth wrote his Highways and Byways in Leicestershire. Of the Enclosure Act, he says (in chapter 7): 'No provision, unhappily, was made for the retention of access to the windy heights of the Charnwood Hills. . . . .the omission is grievously felt now. Of the choicest viewpoints scarcely one is open to the public as of right'.

He lists Bardon Hill, Warren Hills, Broombriggs and Beacon, as closed (because the 'sacred birds of sport must never be disturbed'). All of these are now open to us. We can go up Bardon Hill and over and round the Warren Hills. We can now wander freely on Beacon Hill as well as in Bradgate Park. We have permission to go on paths round Broombriggs Hill and through the Outwoods and over Buck Hill. Many of these were gifts by Victorian or 20th century benefactors for 'the quiet enjoyment of the countryside'. Other land like the Rippin Memorial path was bought by public subscription. Much footpath access has been arranged by local government. County Hall now negotiates public access and provides general footpath management. The Woodland Trust has done much to provide paths through their woods (as in Martinshaw), and is doing something towards reestablishing the woodland of the area by planting many more trees in Ratby Burroughs, for example. It is hoped that the New National Forest will do the same, to improve the wooded landscape and provide new public access on paths within the woodland.

Humbler folk make gifts of seats and trees to show their appreciation of access to the beautiful Charnwood countryside.

This is an area to be cherished and protected for future generations, to be walked with love and gratitude now.

The walks are offered in the hope that you will enjoy them as much I do,   **Heather MacDermid 1996**

ACKNOWLEDGEMENTS

My thanks to the many friends who have encouraged me, with books, with information, with companionship and shared interests. I am grateful for all the informal tutorials I have received!

*liding Stone rocks in Bradgate Park a favourite place for children's hide and seek.
photo. by Philippa Smith)*

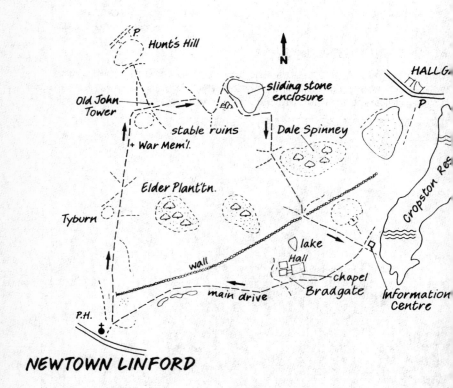

THE DEER PARK AND HALL RUINS
Newtown Linford   Bradgate Park   Old John **1**

'No need to ask whither: where does Leicester spend its holiday but at Bradgate Park.'
W. Napier Reeve (Eliot Roscoe) Bradgate Park: its story and its scenery   1849

Distance 4 miles

How to get there Newtown Linford is about 6 miles NW of Leicester, just north of Anstey

Starting points
From the car park in Bradgate Park, Newtown Linford
Put 50p in the honesty box if you leave your car and make sure you are back by nightfall!

Bus routes Buses to Newtown Linford. Ring Busline.

Refreshment Various cafes and pubs in Newtown Linford which serve food. Ice creams etc usually available in Bradgate carparks..

The route begins with an initial gentle climb up to Tyburn and the war memorial over the rocky volcanic outcrops to reach Old John. We descend from Old John to pass twisted rock formations and walled enclosures and follow a gradual slope down to the information centre and ruins of Bradgate. The main drive makes an easy return route. As this is open country, you can choose your own route back if you prefer to extend the walk, stopping where you will and admiring the views all the way!

Items of interest Bradgate Park, once the deer park of Groby Manor, owned by the Grey family, who became Earls of Stamford. Deer now wander free from the hunt in this quiet parkland. You can sit in peace to admire the views from the many seats, donated in memory of people who have loved the park.

Bennion of Thurnby purchased the park in 1928 from the heirs of the Greys of Groby "in trust for all time to be preserved in its natural state for quiet enjoyment of people of Leicestershire. His true memorial lies all around".

Tyburn, a lovely unfenced spinney, where you might easily meet small deer sheltering. Not a hanging place for humans, despite its London connotations!

Old John, the mug-shaped folly on the hill was built in1784 on the site of an old mill.

The ruins of Bradgate House, the birthplace and home of Lady Jane Grey (1537–1554)

The war memorial built in memory of wartime casualties of wars of 1902 and 1914 stands on an impressive outcrop of sharp pointed rock If you go round to the right of it you can admire its sheer sloping sides and the evidence of sea fossils. (Be very careful not to damage any fossils you see. They are rare in pre Cambrian rock.)

Before you leave the enclosure beyond the memorial, go to the right to see the remaining walls of the old stable block where the 7th Earl of Stamford, kept his racehorses.

The toposcope at Old John was provided by the inhabitants of Newtown Linford from the proceeds of their village pageant in 1952.

The rocky outcrops at the foot of Old John, just beyond the little round pool, near Sliding Stone enclosure, are slump agglomerates, the results of enormous volcanic pressures. Admire the persistence of the lone tree which grows bravely in the clefts of the twisted rock formations.

Country Park Visitors Centre is only open at certain times, between April and October. There is a small charge to enter. The toilets are usually open and well kept and free.

The ruins of Bradgate House, the birthplace and home of Lady Jane Grey (1537–1554). The Grey family became related to the kings of England when Edward IV fell in love with and married Elizabeth Woodville, widow of Sir John Grey. The house was started in 1500 by her son Thomas Grey, first Marquis of Dorset. The fashionable brick house with its fancy diaper patterning was made from local clay. The local peasants were evicted and Thomas Grey was brought to book in Chancery for this illegal act. He claimed that he had rehoused the villagers elsewhere. The lost village of Bradgate is now probably under the reservoir.

The Greys were elevated to the status of Earls of Stamford in 1628. The second earl entertained William III here very lavishly in 1696, built stables for 100 horses and used part of the park as a race course. But he died without direct heirs in 1720. The Stamfords eventually sold the estate to Bennion, who donated it to the people of Leicestershire.

In 1842 Queen Adelaide, the widow of William IV came here for her 50th birthday picnic under the oak in front of the ruins. Many others come here for less extravagant picnics.

THE DEER PARK AND HALL RUINS
Newtown Linford   Bradgate Park   Old John

1. **From Newtown Linford** go through Bradgate carpark and then through the high kissing gates by the main drive. Turn left to cross the main drive and continue with the park wall on your left for a short distance. Strike uphill and keep to the high ridge of the rocky granite outcrop, with the park wall down to your left and the main drive down to your right. (The people on it look very small already!) Go through the gap in the wall ahead and continue uphill.

2. Make for a clump of trees on Tyburn Hill, to the left of the war memorial straight ahead. On the far side of the spinney continue uphill towards the memorial.

3. Go through the gateway of the walled enclosure ahead. On the far side of it Old John monument rises up. Approach Old John, carefully, over the rocks and survey the world around you. The toposcope indicates the places around. We descend the hill in the direction of Burrough Hill and Rothley Plain, due east. Look for a little round pond below you and note the rocky outcrop beyond it, in front of the wall of Sliding Stone walled enclosure.

4. Make your way downhill to pass this round pond and go uphill, leaving the main tracks to reach the rocky outcrop. Sliding Stone plantation wall is in front of us.

5. Make your way round to the right of Sliding Stone Enclosure. When the wall on your left ends, keep in the same direction to reach the cliff edge of the sharp pointed, slatey rocks. Look down on the ruins of Bradgate House with its triangular lake beside it. This is our next goal, but we pass to the left of it to reach the Visitors Centre first.

6. Below the cliffs, on each side of the House there are walled spinneys, the circular coppice of Bowling Green Spinney on your right and wall of Dale Spinney on your left. Follow the wall of Dale Spinney until it curves left to go uphill and then make your way downhill, aiming for the left of the ruins and the lake. A gap in the wall enables you to walk between the lake enclosure on your right and Deer Park spinney on your left..

7. Pass the Keepers house over to your left and continue to the Country Park Visitors Centre and toilets ahead.

8. You are now on the main drive through Bradgate park, between Hallgates car park and the main Newtown Linford car park . Follow the main drive to pass the ruins to return to Newtown Linford, where the

walk started. (If you want to add on the 3 mile Cropston Reservoir circuit, you can turn left when you reach the ruins of the house.) The carpark is only a mile further along the drive from the ruins to Newtown Linford.

A GREAT HALL, A RESERVOIR AND A LOST, DROWNED VILLAGE

2

Hallgates   Bradgate Ruins   Cropston

'First I cam oute of Brodegate Parke into the Forest of Charley, commonly callid the wast. This forest is XX miles or more in cumpace, having plenty of woode and the most parte of it at this time longgith to the marquise of Dorset: the residue to the King and Erle of Hunting dune. In this forest is no good toune nor scant a village . . .'
John Leland   1540

Distance 4½ miles

Starting points Hall Gates car park, near Cropston, by the reservoir dam. (Pay and Display car park ticket 50p)
It is possible to start this walk from Cropston or from the ruins of Bradgate House, if you wish to add it onto the Newtown Linford and Bradgate Park walk.

How to get there Cropston is 4½ miles NW of Leicester. Follow the B5330 road signposted from Cropston to Woodhouse Eaves. The car park is the first turn left after the reservoir dam. There are occasional buses which pass through Cropston.

Refreshment The Reservoir Hotel and Bradgate Arms pubs at Cropston both serve food. The Bradgate Arms is 400 years old. The Reservoir Hotel was once the manor house, where a Mr Billy Booten served food and drink from a shed to the navvies working on the reservoir.

The route From the car park at Hallgates you can wander anywhere in the park. The main drive, on flat ground, leads straight through to Newtown Linford past the ruins of Bradgate Hall . We leave the main drive and take a more adventurous hilly route through Bradgate Park, but do go as far as or as high as Old John. We come down by Bowling Green Spinney with fine views of the reservoir below, to pass the ruins of Bradgate House. The next section of the walk is on flat ground beside the reservoir to Cropston. You may have to cross a ploughed field here, but the route is mainly on grassland or on headland paths.

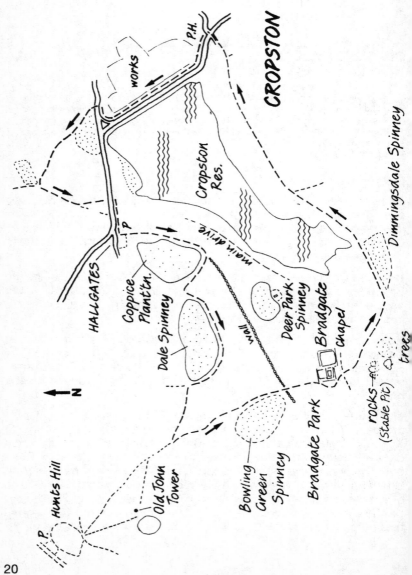

From Cropston village (where you can have a pub stop) there is half a mile of road walking over the dam and then you can choose to leave the road and walk a greener route for the short distance back to Hallgates.

Items of interest Cropston reservoir was built in 1866 and flooded about 200 acres. The lost village of Bradgate is somewhere under the waters. The people were turned out and resettled in Newtown Linford when Grey, the Marquis of Dorset, built his stately house in the park. As you admire the lovely views over the reservoir give a thought to the displaced peasants and to the lost farms drowned by the reservoir in Victorian times. Their loss is our gain. Water birds abound here. Take your binoculars as well as your camera!

Bradgate House is an ancient monument, open to the public on certain days in summer months. Think of Lady Jane Grey, happily studying Latin and Greek here, while her relatives went out hunting in the park. The only roofed part of the building is the old chapel, which now houses the remaining monuments.
Peacocks can usually be heard and seen near the ruins.

Cropston village has no church, as it is part of the hamlet of Thurcaston, but it has a fine Free Church chapel, dated 1850.

A GREAT HALL, A RESERVOIR AND A LOST, DROWNED VILLAGE
Hallgates   Bradgate Ruins   Cropston

1. **From Hallgates car park (near Old John, Bradgate Park)** go diagonally uphill, between the park drive and the park wall which goes off to your right. Aim for the wall of Coppice Plantation on the hill. (Stop for breath at the little rocky outcrop and admire the view over the reservoir.)

2. Keep the plantation wall on your right. Practise your mountaineering skills on the short rocky scramble to join a good track which curves you further round the plantation. Go through the wall gap. (This wall goes downhill and bends to form a very long straight wall which passes the back of the Bradgate House ruins. You will cross it later, near Bowling Green Spinney.)

3. Continue with Coppice Plantation on your right until you meet a main track which leads you left, to the next walled woodland, Dale Spinney.

4. Pass Dale Spinney on your right. Follow the curve of the wall. Old John and the war memorial come into view ahead.. Turn left on any of

One of the Bradgate Park's pollarded oaks, with Tyburn Spinney beyond. (photo. by Philippa Smith)

the many tracks, to cross the valley (leaving Old John up on the hill to the right) and meet Bowling Green Spinney.

5. Turn left again to keep Bowling Green Spinney wall on your right and go downhill on the main track which goes straight past the ruins of the hall. Go through the wide gap in the long straight wall and walk close to the wall which encloses the house and the lake on your left. Meet the drive. The walk continues in this direction, over the drive and crossing the bridge over the river Lin.

6. Bradgate ruins: pause here to admire the building. Newtown Linford lies along the drive, to your right. The Country Park Visitors Centre and toilets are to your left along the drive. The bridge over the little River Lin lies ahead.

7. **From Bradgate House Ruins** cross the main drive, and go over the bridge. Stable Pit rock formation rises, like a beached whale, from a hollow on your right near a junction of three tracks. The main track bends right, the middle goes to Anstey.

8. Swing left on the faint track which goes, parallel with the river over to your left, towards Dimmingsdale Spinney. A kissing gate beside the big fence gate in the left corner of the park brings you out with the paling of Cropston reservoir on your left.

9. Keep Dimmingsdale spinney on your right. At the narrow end of the field, a stile leads onto a little fenced off path, close to the wood on your right (to keep you away from the worst of the mud here.) Keep in the same direction, close to Cropston reservoir on your left, with a big field sloping up on your right. Follow the hedge on your left and go through the the wide gateway in the top corner.

10. Keep in the same direction, along the good track, close to the hedge now on your right. Join the hedged farm lane which leads into Causeway Lane, Cropston. (Pass several attractive old cottages here, timber and old brick, thatched or slated.)

11. Meet the crossroads of Station Road Cropston. (The Bradgate Arms pub lies 100 paces along Station Road and the journey is worth the effort. You pass many very pretty old houses.)

12. **From Cropston to Hallgates car park** take the main road, signposted to Bradgate. Pass The Reservoir pub on your right. You now have half a mile of road walking, but there is a proper pavement and there are fine views of the reservoir, with many water birds to entertain and delight you. The road is the high dam of the reservoir. The Victorian water works are well hidden down to your right, beyond the hedge, in fine grounds with tall conifer trees.

13. At the road junction at the end of the dam, the main road goes left to Hallgates car park but if you prefer a field path, which makes a short extension to the walk, fork right on the minor road signposted to Swithland. Pass the triangular section of wood on your left.

14. Turn right along Bradgate Road for 50 paces and turn left at the footpath sign opposite the big house.

15. Walk along the track at the edge of the spinney. Continue with the hedge on your right, past a bulrushy pond in the narrow end of the field. Keep in the same direction, still with the hedge on your right. The route becomes a narrow (and sometimes muddy) fenced-off path between barbed wire and thorny hedges as it passes various paddock fields. (Take care, and complain to the management if you find it damaging or dangerous!)

16. Turn left at the main track from Swithland woods to Hallgates. It meets the road as a bridleway, but you can fork right on a signposted footpath which goes across two small fields and comes out on the road a little nearer to Hallgates car park.

The main drive through the park leads to Newtown Linford, two miles away

THE SWITHLAND SLATE TRAIL
Hunts Hill Car Park (Bradgate Park)
Woodhouse Eaves   Swithland Woods

3

'No one who goes to Bradgate but what climbs the hill to Old John'
W. Napier Reeve (Eliot Roscoe) Bradgate Park: its story and its scenery 1849

Distance 5½ miles

Starting points Hunts Hill car park (50p in honesty box).
or Woodhouse Eaves
Toilets in car parks

How to get there Hunts Hill car park is north of Newtown Linford, 2 miles by road or 1½ miles by foot through Bradgate Park.

Bus routes. Regular bus services to Newtown Linford and Woodhouse Eaves. Ring Busline for details.

Refreshment Various good pubs which serve food in Woodhouse Eaves. (I can recommend the Pear Tree, Routier Guide. Coffee a little upmarket in price, but pleasant and welcoming ambience!) Ye Olde

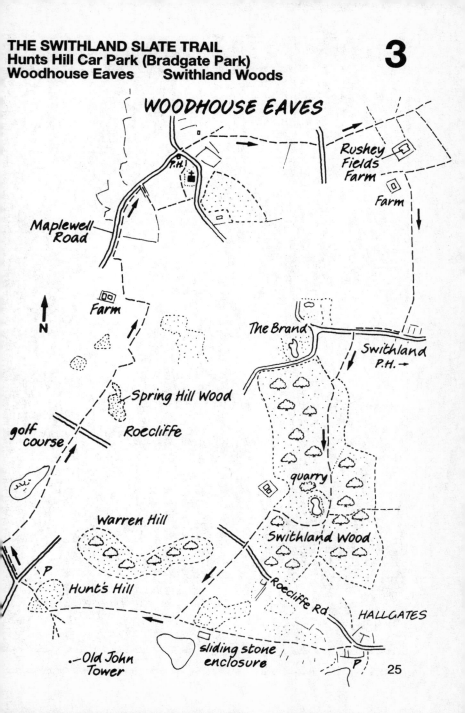

WOODHOUSE EAVES

P.H.

Rushey
Fields
Farm

Farm

Maplewell
Road

Farm

N

The Brand

Swithland
P.H. →

Spring Hill Wood

Roecliffe

golf
course

quarry

Warren Hill

Swithland Wood

Hunt's Hill

P

Roecliffe Rd

HALLGATES

Old John
Tower

sliding stone
enclosure

P

25

Woodhouse Eaves church which stands impressively on Forest Rock, a location for rock climber

Bulls Head is at the other end of the village and is popular for food. Ice creams etc in the car parks in Bradgate.

The route Over the golf course and through fields and downhill into the pretty village of Woodhouse, with its thatched and Swithland-slated roofs. Then over farmland, mainly on good headland paths well walked and waymarked. Due south to the fringes of Swithland, (the pub and church are a mile away along the road). The walk through Swithland Woods is always delightful. It doesn't matter which path you take but, for those who worry about being lost in forests, the route described here enables you to see the deep disused slate quarry and to find your way out by a minor path. The wood, though small, can be quite confusing,

Items of interest. Our route passes close to Woodhouse Eaves church which stands impressively on a rock above a cave of an old quarry. It was, like the Copt Oak and the Oaks in Charnwood churches, built at the time of the Enclosure. Designed by William Railton (of Nelson's Column fame) it was built in 1837. It is a very impressive setting. Note the number of houses in the village with Swithland slate roofs.

Swithland Woods were quarried for slate in Roman times. Swithland slates have been found in Roman buildings in Leicester and in Lincoln. Records show that in the 13th century they were used in Beaumanor Hall and in the 14th century in Leicester Castle. They are much valued as roofing material and make many a house picturesque. They are much in evidence in local churchyards and there was a whole school of slate inscribers in the 18th century. Slates were transported to London by canal. St Pancras Hotel was roofed and pavemented on one side with Swithland slates and the other with Groby 'grey' slates. It was only when the import of thinner Welsh slates became cheap because of improved national transport that the industry declined. The woods and the quarry were purchased by the Rotary club for the enjoyment of the public.

THE SWITHLAND SLATE TRAIL
Hunts Hill Car Park (Bradgate Park)   Woodhouse Eaves Swithland Woods

1. **From the car park at Hunts Hill** cross the road and continue towards Shepshed on the B5330, Benscliffe Road.

2. Turn right at the footpath sign into the second field. Walk close to the hedge on your right. The route goes to the bottom left corner of the

27

field, past a rocky outcrop over to your left. (But the farmer usually leaves a good headland for people who wish to walk round the edge of the field to reach this point.) Cross through the stiled field corner and walk with the hedge on your left across the Lingdale golf course, to reach the road (Joe Moore's Lane).

3. Cross the road carefully to continue in the same direction beside the golf course, close to the hedge on your right. The route across the golf course is usually well signed. (In the corner of the field, to the right of the fairway, pass the rocky outcrop of Spring Hill Wood. You need to keep in the same direction, but make a detour right, along an old line of trees and then after 50 yards bear left round a small copse of trees. Keep the hedge on your left until you come to the stile and slate bridge which takes you into the corner of a field, with Maplewell farm in the far left corner.)

4. The path continues to the corner of the field just to the right of Maplewell farm buildings. (Turn right and left round two sides of the field to reach this point.) Pass under the telegraph wires and cross the stile. Follow the hedge on your left. Keep in the same direction, joining the gravel track which comes from Barn Farm. This bends left to meet Maplewell Road.

5. Turn right along Maplewell Road and walk downhill into Woodhouse Eaves. Pass the entrance to the Broombriggs farm trail on your left and continue downhill until you reach the Mill Lane/ Victoria Road crossing. (Meadow Lane crossroads is at the foot of the hill, but to see the church we make a little detour.)

6. Turn right and walk up Victoria Road, steeply uphill to the granite arch at the top. Meet the track and turn left along the tarmac strip. Just before you reach the road, turn left through a wooden gate and walk into a narrow grassy field. Go steeply downhill, close to the hedge on the left. Join the fenced track which swings right. Pass Woodhouse Eaves church on your right and emerge on Church Hill road opposite a big garage. Two pubs are on your left, the Forest Rock and the Pear Tree. Meadow Lane is on your right.

7. **From Woodhouse Eaves** cross-roads, follow Meadow Lane. Pass the primary school on your left and swing right almost immediately, to cross the footpath stile. The path is usually left as a clear raised strip across ploughed field. It joins a headland, close to a hedge on your right, and meets the road. The tall silos of Rushey Fields stand ahead.

8. Cross the road and follow the Leicestershire Round waymark signs, with the hedge on your left for three fields. Cross the farm-drive from Rushey Fields farm on your right and continue for one more field.

Cross the Private Road and turn right at the end of the field. Pass the farm over to your right. Go uphill to meet the lane.

. Turn right to pass Rushall Fields Farm then turn left at the footpath sign (to Swithland).

0. Follow the hedge on your left. Cross the wooden fence and move slightly right to reach the bottom corner of the field. As you go downhill note the hedge in front of you. It leads straight to Swithland.

1. Cross the footbridge in the bottom right corner of the field and merge with this marker hedge on your left. Follow it all the way to the main street which runs through Swithland. (The Griffin pub lies about three quarters of a mile to the left but our path turns right.)

2. **From Swithland** follow the main street (away from The Griffin pub) towards Bradgate and Woodhouse. Turn left at the de-restriction sign on a hedged path beside a slate house (Woodlane Cottage).

3. This track leads straight into Swithland Woods. The main path follows the yellow markers of the bridleway and crosses a little open triangular glade, with a railed off water pump on your right. It then dips down to cross an insignificant stream and rises to a high point where you have the old quarry pool paling fence up on your right.

4 To see the rocky face of the old slate quarry you need to climb up to the paling fence which surrounds the deep quarry pool. Take care. It is fenced off because it is so deep and steep sided. You can walk all the way round the pool until you reach this main track again.

5. The main drive continues in a southerly direction towards Bradgate but we turn right, just after the quarry pool. A track leads off at right angles (due west). Follow this minor path until you reach the wall at the far edge of the wood (near the Swithland holiday home chalets).

6. Turn left, just inside the wood and continue close to the wall on your right (due south again).

7. Meet the road and cross to the footpath sign opposite. Old John stands impressively ahead of you. Walk up the good track, past the reservoir filter station on your left, and enter the park through the high kissing gate. Turn right.

8. You do not need to climb the hill to Old John to reach Hunts Hill car park. You can follow the park wall and go through the next kissing gate. The car park lies just past the toilets, in the spinney.

SLATES AND GRIFFINS
Hallgates   The Brand   Swithland Woods   4

Charnwood Forest, a tract some five miles by four, a mountain region in miniature
Paget and Irvine   County Books Leicestershire

Distance about 5½ miles. Short circuit, omitting Rabbits Bridge, 3½ miles.

Starting points Hallgates car park near Cropston. Car park has toilets. Swithland has street parking only. The Griffin pub might give you permission to park if you plan to eat there.

How to get there Hallgates car park entrance to Bradgate Park is on the B5330 from Leicester via Anstey and Cropston.
Swithland is north of Cropston, between Woodhouse Eaves and Rothley.

Bus routes To Hallgates, near Cropston and to Swithland. 122, 123 buses go hourly at times. Ring Busline

Refreshment The Griffin Inn at Swithland (but don't rely on it. It seems to change hands a lot. Ring first to check.)

The route Easy tracks through the beautiful Swithland Woods, some optional little climbs up to see the deep old quarry pools. A stop in Swithland for those who want a short cut. A loop through gentle farmland and along a country lane to Rabbits Bridge then farmland fields back to Swithland. Flat track back to Hallgates. Occasional muddy bits. Lovely views everywhere.
In February I saw snowdrops, yellow hammers, chaffinches and merrily tooting steam trains.

Items of interest Swithland Woods slate quarries, used in Roman times, now taken over by nature and police deep divers. Purchased by the Rotary Club in 1931.
Griffins in Swithland. The school has a stone griffin and date of 1843 over the porch. The pub is called the Griffin. Note the round tower of the little lockup.
Swithland church is only a little way beyond The Griffin. Largely modern with ancient memorials, it has a perkily pinnacled little tower and fascinating tombs to the Danvers (1745) and the Hinds (1840) and stones to members of the Bunney family and tombs to the Danvers family in the churchyard. The story is told of a much loved dog buried outside the churchyard, as regulations decreed, but close to the churchyard wall to be near its master's tomb.

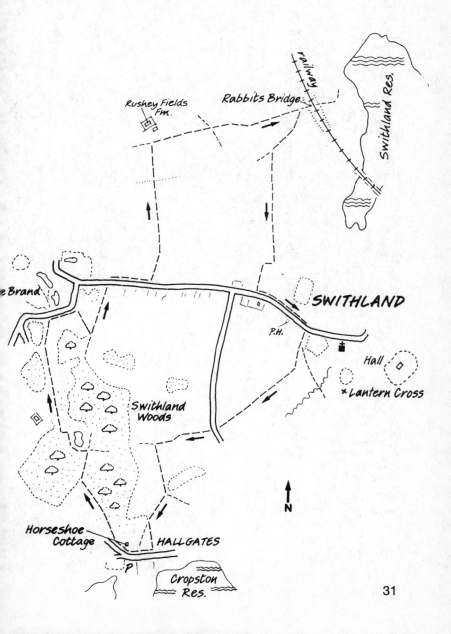

A view over the blue waters of Swithland Woods quarry pool.

Swithland Hall, once home of the Earl of Lanesborough.

The Brand, long the home of the Martin family. Many scouts and guides have been welcomed here.

Great Central railway, a lovingly restored line, with steam trains at weekends throughout the year and on high days and holidays.

SLATES AND GRIFFINS

Hallgates   The Brand   Swithland Woods

From Hallgates car park turn left along the road, curving round the dangerous bend by Horse Shoe cottage. Ignore the bridleway into Bradgate Park on your left .

1. Cross the road carefully to the footpath sign by the big slate stone farm buildings.

2. Cross the stile by the (muddy) gateway and go diagonally left in the big meadow. In the far corner cross the good footplank bridge over the stream and enter Swithland Woods.

3. Turn left to meet the main track through the woods, which comes from the road. Turn right to follow this slatey stony track uphill for about 30 paces. (Yellow marker posts show that it is a bridleway.)

4. Swing left to go uphill to the wooden paling fencing which encircles the old slate quarry. Keep on the high ground and make a big semi-circle round the pool. Stop to look across the water when you have a good clear view of the inscribed slab on the far side, mirrored in the water. This tells you the area was procured by the Rotary Club.

5. Continue to the corner of the paling. You can see the main track, over to your right but this time we go left. Go steeply downhill to meet a good track and turn left, (past a seat to the memory of Sarah and Joseph Saer, A Loving Couple). The green holiday chalets of Swithland encampment can be seen ahead on raised ground. Aim for the corner of the wall surrounding them.

6. Go through the gap in the wall and walk along the slate walled drive past the camp. This drive meets the road to Roecliffe. If at any point you prefer to walk in the woods, simply turn right and follow any little woodland path parallel with this drive wall.

7. At the road we turn right, but you can keep inside the woods, keeping the road wall over to your left.
When you reach the entrance drive into the little car park, it is well worth going to the road and crossing it, carefully, just to see the spectacularly beautiful old slate quarry of the Brand hills. Here the

steep-sided slabs rise vertically from a very pretty pool dappled with light from lovely woodland and alive with fish and bulrushes. The beauty is deceptive however: do not attempt to approach. The pool is dangerous and the land is private. Return to the wood across the road.)

8. Continue in the same direction and meet the fence of another quarry, inside the wood. You can climb the little hill to look at it through the paling fence, but it is small dark and forbidding.

9. Keep the paling on your left and then follow the wall.
(From this high point you have good views across the whole valley looking down on Quorn, Barrow, Buddon Hill and Swithland. When trains are running the line of the railway can be detected by the little puffs of steam.)

10. Look down at the open field just outside the wood. It is bordered by the walled track which takes you into Swithland. To reach it, go downhill to meet a track, turn right and then turn left by the gate and stile which lead into this little narrow walled track. Follow the track onto the road, near Woodlane Cottage.

11. Turn right, along the main street. Swithland church and the Griffin pub lie straight ahead. We turn left on a loop to Rabbits Bridge, to see the steam trains and the viaduct. (If you want a short cut you can go straight to the pub, omitting the next section 12–20.)

From Swithland to Rabbits Bridge and the reservoir
12. Pass Chapel End and the bus stop and turn left at the footpath sign by the house called Mole End. Go uphill with the hedge on your right.
  From the high ground you have fine views of Charnwood hills to your left and of Buddon Hill in the Soar valley to your right. Swithland Reservoir is only visible in winter, when the trees are leafless, but you can probably hear the little trains tooting away as they cross it. Over to your left the little white houses and the big impressive chapel of Woodhouse Eaves can be seen. The landscape changes to a more agrarian one, of ploughed field and pasture.
Ahead stand the tall silos of Rushey Fields farm, our next goal.

13. Cross the fencing at the end of the field and go through the patch of woodland. Then make your way diagonally uphill to meet the hedge on your right. Follow it to the footpath sign just to the right of Rushey Fields farm buildings.

14. Turn right along the lane. Pass Rushall Fields farm (with slate roof and slate stone base) on your right and continue along the lane admiring the views. (The big white house over to your left is Garats

Hay, with its distinctive little pointy spire. The even bigger one over to your right is Swithland Hall.) Ignore the bridleways to left and right. When the lane dips down to a hollow you have a good view of the railway line across your route. Continue uphill towards the railway bridge.

15. Note the footpath sign on your right. This is your return route, but it is difficult to resist the temptation to continue to the railway bridge to look at the trains and to go a bit further along the lane to see the reservoir and the long viaduct over which the trains cross. A lovely spot to pause, watch the birds, take photos or eat or drink whatever you have in your rucsac. Return to the footpath sign.

From Rabbits Bridge to Swithland

16. From the footpath sign downhill from the railway bridge go down the steepsided wooded bank (taking care you don't slip). Walk close to the hedge and stream on your right. Follow the hedge for three more fields.

17. From the gate at the end of the third field, stop to look diagonally left. The big white building of Swithland Hall stands out dramatically against a dark background of conifer trees.

18. Keep the hedge on your right to the next corner. Cross what is usually a very dirty, wet track. A stile takes you to a little fenced off path round the corner of the worst bit.

19. Turn left in the next field and continue close to the hedge on your left. Go downhill to meet the main street in Swithland, opposite number 140, Candlemass Cottage.

20. Turn left. Pass the school and the Griffin pub and continue to the bridleway sign at the bend of the road. (Continue along the road for a short distance to see the village church.)

21. From the bridleway sign at the bend in the road, follow the (usually muddy) path beside the little water works shed and cross the stream. Follow the wall and hedge on your right.

22. Two paths fork in this field. The footpath to your left goes to Thurcaston. (You could go a little way along it for a distant glimpse of the old lantern cross in the grounds.) We take the bridleway to Swithland Woods and Hallgates. Go across the open end of the field and through the handgate. Old John is directly in front of you.

23. Follow the stony track (beside old isolated trees and occasional big boulders). Meet the road.

24. Cross to the bridleway opposite. This begins as a drive to

Cropston Leys. Pass the sheds, house and conifer edged garden on your left and continue on the track, with Swithland Woods straight ahead. We do not go quite as far as the woods, but turn left at a main path junction.

25. Walk beside a line of old trees, halfway between Swithland Wood on your right and the conifers of Cropston Leys over to your left. Follow this well walked path into the corner of the wood ahead. (But do look back to see how far away Swithland Hall now looks. It is one of the fascinations of walking to see how distances in a landscape move and change!)

26. Follow the good (but sometimes muddy) track through the wood. Keep in this direction (parallel with the edge of Swithland Wood over to your right).

27. Meet the road and turn right to Hallgates car park.

NED LUDD, THE NAVVIES AND CROPSTON RESERVOIR

5

Anstey   Cropston

> **William III . . . rode from Leicester to Anstey, the land then being unenclosed**
> Companion to Charnwood Forest   1858

Distance 3 miles (or 4 miles from the centre of Anstey)

Starting points Anstey, Cropston
The walk could be started from either end. If you start from Cropston you can omit Anstey. If you start from Anstey centre you have to be interested in urban vernacular architecture and industrial development to enjoy the walk through streets uphill to reach Anstey Martin High school.

How to get there From Leicester follow Anstey Lane and signs into Anstey. Cropston can be reached by following the B5328 from Anstey or from the A6 via Rothley.

Car parking Public car park close to Anstey centre roundabout, behind shops Some street parking in the wide streets near Anstey Martin school. (This shortens the walk.)
No public carparks at Cropston.

Bus routes Ring Busline for details. Service 74 and 121 from Beaumont Leys

Anstey   Cropston

5

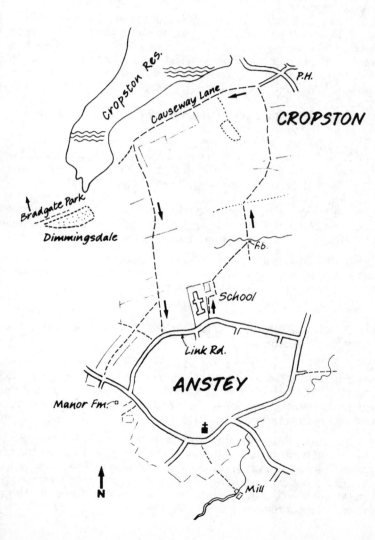

Refreshment Pubs at Cropston serve food.
There is a tea shop in Anstey as well as pubs and shops.

The route An easy, short walk between two villages on the edge of Charnwood. Fine views of Bradgate. The walk can be added onto the next walk which includes the more beautiful route to Bradgate.

Items of interest
Anstey was a Saxon settlement. Recorded as Hanstige, the high path, in Domesday Book, it is an example of one of those villages in Leicestershire where the H has been dropped! (It is interesting to note that Richard Cobbet spells Aylestone as 'Hailstone' in his Rural Rides, 1830. He obviously presumed it was really spelt with an initial h, having decided that Leicester people always dropped their aitches!)
The village has a fine packhorse bridge which was used until recent times when the new road was built.
Ned Ludd, the village idiot, gave his name to the Luddite movement which broke up machines which were putting frameknitters out of work in the early 19th century, at the time of the Napoleonic wars.
Manor Farm is the oldest building. It stands near the brick pinfold on the Green.
There are traces of Norman building in the tower and the stump of a Saxon preaching cross in the churchyard but the church is mainly rebuilt (1845). The stone is Mountsorrel granite.

Cropston has no church but has a big chapel and a pub which is 400 years old. The Reservoir pub was once the manor house and served drink to the navvies who built the reservoir.

NED LUDD, THE NAVVIES AND CROPSTON RESERVOIR
Anstey   Cropston

From Anstey town centre roundabout, walk up any of the town streets to reach the Martin High School or follow Bradgate Road, signposted to Newtown Linford, passing the church on your right to reach the Green and the pinfold. Turn right to follow Link Road to reach the Martin High school. (Link Road is a very long road for pedestrians!)

1. **From the Anstey Martin High school** on Link Road, pass the school buildings on your left and walk up the wide drive between houses. The drive bends sharp right, past the school yard and playing fields. Cross the stile and turn left with the rugby field on your right. (Spectacular views ahead over to Bradgate and Charnwood, with old John and the war memorial clearly visible.)

2. At the end of the school fencing go diagonally right downhill through a little plantation of trees and continue through scrubby ground down to the stream on your left. Cross the big slate bridge and continue uphill close to the hedge on your left. (Good wide, open views over to Castle Hill Beamont Leys. No castle now, just a huge factory building on the hill.)

3. Cross a track and move slightly right on a well trodden path (usually between crops). Go slightly downhill to the next waymarked crossing (a wide double guillotine gate beside a long concrete stile.) Go uphill for two fields, with the hedge on your right, to reach Causeway Lane. (Cropston village, with pubs, lies to your right)

4. Turn left at Causeway Lane, Cropston.

From Cropston walk along Causeway Lane and continue on the wide stony track. Keep in the same direction, through the waymarked gate and follow the hedge on your left, with Cropston reservoir down on your right. Here you can relax and savour the views as you go along the easy track.

5. When the drive bends left, just before the field dips down towards the reservoir, go through the gateway and continue close to the hedge on your left, with the reservoir behind you.

6. This headland bridleway takes you straight back to Anstey Martin school. The view ahead is not particularly attractive, so make sure you keep turning back, to look at the Charnwood Hills, Bradgate Park and the keeper's house by the reservoir. The track is easily followed. It becomes a narrowly fenced off path which is invariably muddy and unattractive as you near the school and the houses. (Halfway up the fenced path it is possible to turn right to go across the field as a short cut if you intend to add on the next walk. See the map.)

7. Link Road, with telephone box and bus stop, lies straight ahead. The Martin High school is to your left and Anstey town centre straight ahead, (via Dalby road and Hollow Road.) If you wish to add on the next walk turn right and walk down Forest Gate to reach Bradgate Road, emerging opposite the old pinfold on the Green by Manor Farm.

A ROYAL PICNIC
Anstey   Bradgate   Newtown Linford

"Ah! the old woman was right that bade us take this road"
W. Napier Reeve (Eliot Roscoe) Bradgate Park: its story and its scenery   1849

Distance 4 miles

Starting points Anstey Green, Bradgate Road, Anstey or Newtown Linford
The walk could be started from either end or added onto the previous walk.

How to get there From Leicester follow Anstey Lane and signs to Anstey and continue along Bradgate Road towards Newtown Linford until you reach the green.

Car parking Public carpark close to Anstey centre roundabout, behind shops
Newtown Linford has a big carpark, with toilets, at Bradgate.

Bus routes From a bus going to Newtown Linford, get off at the Top Green (near Manor Farm, Anstey) or continue to Newtown Linford.

Refreshment Pubs at Newtown Linford or pots of tea and cakes at one of the cafes to set you up for the return journey? Or a picnic in Bradgate park, where Queen Adelaide picnicked? Anstey, less picturesque, has a cafe, pubs and shops.

The route Easy and pleasant walking. Fine views as you approach Bradgate Park from Anstey. Some stiles to cross. Some arable fields, but the paths are usually well cleared. Some can be muddy in places in wet weather. The route goes along the main drive of the park, beside interesting rocks, old trees and the pretty little River Lin. As you walk along the road from Newtown Linford you can look over the wall on your left at the marvellous views over Bradgate Park to Cropston reservoir.
From Newtown Linford we approach the valley of Leicester. Flatter country lies ahead. You can see County Hall, sailing like a white liner in green countryside and further in the distance, Billesdon Coplow, a rounded hill with its distinctive cleft, can usually be seen.

Items of interest
Newtown Linford is a most attractive tourist spot, with several cruck cottages and picturesque thatching. The church, charmingly set by the little River Lin, has a Swithland slate roof and fine Swithland slate gravestones.
There is a well stocked post office shop and good cafes and pubs.

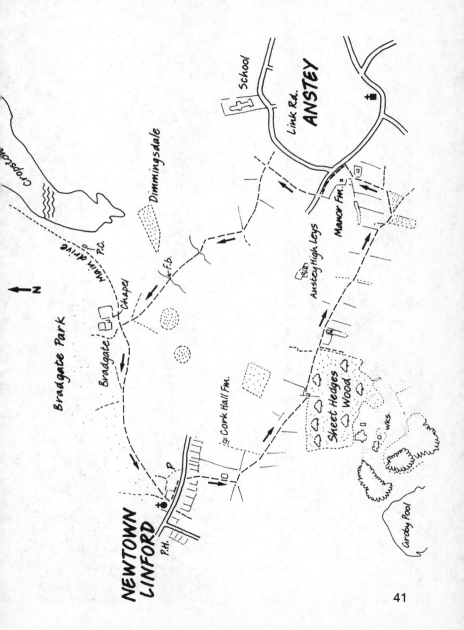

The beautiful Groby Pool, site of Special Scientific Interest.

Bradgate Park ruins. Queen Adelaide, the widow of William IV picnicked under the tree in front of the ruins in July 1842, on venison, trout and crayfish! (What have you got in your rucsac?)

See the previous walk for details of Anstey.

A ROYAL PICNIC
Anstey   Bradgate   Newtown Linford

From Anstey follow Bradgate Road towards Newtown Linford, passing the church on your right. Pass Anstey Top Green and Manor farm on your left and Forest Gate on your right.

1. Turn right at the waymarked bridleway sign by no 191 Bradgate Road. A handgate leads you into a lovely long straight open field, with a well walked path going straight between old ridges and furrows. At the end of the old field boundary, where the ridges and furrows change direction, cross the ditch and the remains of the old hedge line. (Anstey Martin school is ahead of you and the short cut from the previous walk comes in here)

2. Turn sharp left and follow a hedge on your left. There is a good headland and fine views. Keep in the same direction across the open field corner. Cross the stile and swing slightly right to go towards Old John and the war memorial. There is usually a wide green track between crops. Cross the cart bridge. In the corner of the field you have a beautiful view of the Bradgate House ruins.

3. Cross the waymarked stiles at each end of a steep little trackway (Be careful! It can be slippery) and go through the kissing gates in the park wall ahead.

4. Follow the track through the park to the ruins and turn left along the main drive to reach Newtown Linford.

From Newtown Linford walk along the road towards Leicester, passing Marion's Cottage and the old Sunday school on your left. Ignore the footpath sign on your right (by the sign for house no 522). Ignore the private road to Cork Hall farm on your right.

5. At the de-restriction sign by the end of the houses (where the park wall swings left), turn right at the footpath sign and pass house number 400.

6. Follow the wide drive past houses and then swing left on the (muddy) farm track. Pass big farm sheds on your right and continue to the corner of Sheet Hedges Wood. Turn left, (ignoring the path which

goes down past the wood to Groby). Walk along the plateau of high ground, with Groby down to your right and County Hall ahead of you.

7. Keep close to the hedge on your right. Go through the rough ground which is all that remains of old farmbuildings and continue with the hedge now on your left. Keep straight on to pass Anstey High Leys farm over to your left. The next gateway is a bit to the right of the field corner. Continue close to the hedge on your left, going gently downhill on a good headland. Keep in the same direction across the open field. In the far left corner cross a stile.

8. Two paths fork here. Take the left fork, still close to the hedge on your left. Meet a track and swing left through the narrow funnel end of field. Again, two paths fork. Take the left fork (marked as parish centenary path). Cross stiles and enter a pretty, interestingly varied field, with ridge and fiurrow and a line of old trees.

9. Go downhill close to the hedge on your right, passing the farm yard of Manor Farm. Go through the kissing gate on your right and cross Anstey Top Green, passing the pinfold opposite Forest Gate.

10. To return to the centre of Anstey turn right along Bradgate Road for a quarter of a mile.

INTO THE PARK
Groby   Newtown Linford   Bradgate   7

> 'A quarter of a mile (from Groby) . . . there is as faire and large a pool as lightly is in Leyrcestershire'
> John Leland, 1540

Distance 5 and half miles or 6 miles if you include the optional extra loop through Bradgate Park.

Starting points The walk can be started from either village.
Start from Groby if you like your refreshment break half way round. There is a fine choice of cafes and pub at Newtown Linford or you can go into Bradgate Park for a picnic. Another advantage of starting from Groby is the historical satisfaction of moving out from Groby Old Hall and castle site, the home of the Greys of Groby, into Bradgate Park, where they hunted and where they built their fine new house in fashionable new brick. It is psychologically satisfying, too, to walk away from the noise and bustle of the fast roads near Groby into the peace and quiet of Charnwood.

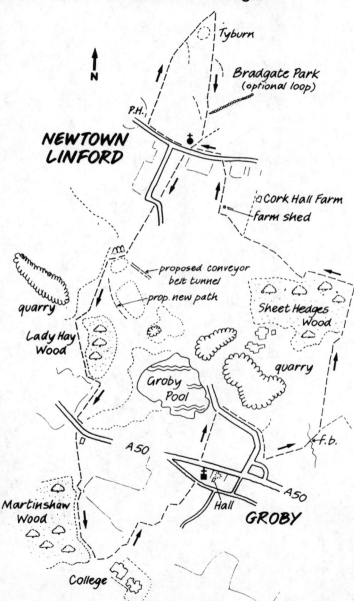

Tyburn

Bradgate Park
(optional loop)

P.H.

NEWTOWN
LINFORD

Cork Hall Farm
farm shed

proposed conveyor
belt tunnel
prop. new path

quarry

Sheet Hedges
Wood

Lady Hay
Wood

Groby
Pool

quarry

A 50

f.b.

Hall

GROBY

A 50

Martinshaw
Wood

College

On the way to Lady Hay Wood, through typical Charnwood landscape.

How to get there From Leicester follow the A50 and the signs into Groby village or follow Anstey Lane and go through Anstey to Newtown Linford.

Parking In Groby there is a car park at the shops opposite Rookery Lane and a public car park next to the Co-op. There is a wide road near Groby church but this is a bus route, and you need to park discreetly.
There is a good car park and picnic site near Groby Pool and this makes a good start to the walk, if you do not mind missing the church and castle site and shops of Groby.
In Newtown Linford you can park in Bradgate Park (but be back before dusk).

Bus routes Both villages are served by buses. Ring Busline for details.

Refreshment Two cafes and pubs in Newtown Linford.
The Earl of Stamford pub in Groby.

The route
The beauty of this walk is doubly precious because of the encroachment of ARC quarries and the new roads, built with material taken from the heart of Charnwood.
(The J92 path, near Newtown Linford, is now vulnerable to ARC quarry operations. A conveyor belt tunnel is planned to go under the track. Let us hope it does not spoil this very beautiful section of the walk.)
The landscape will doubtless change. A new path is planned, (to compensate in part for the disturbance of the quarry operations) in section 12 . This will swing left at the outcrop of rocks and go down through trees to meet the main track which swings left along the lovely valley. It will emerge at Groby Pool. It should be well waymarked and well walked by the time you read this! And it will make a useful short cut for anyone wishing to return straight to Groby Pool car park.
At the moment the J92 track goes into the loveliest field in Leicestershire. It winds down between outcrops of rocks in grassy mounds to a birchwood at the foot of the hill.

Near Newtown Linford the paths are not cleared as they should be, and you may have to walk around the edges of fields. In one place the footpath is very meanly fenced off with barbed wire.
The half mile extra loop through Bradgate Park is delightful.

Items of interest There was a Norman castle in Groby before 1100 and a deer park as long ago as 1288. The only visible remains of Groby motte and bailey castle site now consist of a neglected little domed hump in a field at the back of the beautiful old manor house. The castle was owned by William de Ferrars, in 1273 and Groby was the home of the de Ferrars family who became, by marriage, the Greys of Groby.

An unusual view into Bradgate Park, with Newtown Linford church below.

Elizabeth de Ferrars succeeded her grandfather and married Sir John Grey. She married Edward IV in 1453 and became queen of England. Her sons built Bradgate house in about 1501. Lady Jane Grey, one of her descendants, became a claimant to the throne through her.)

Groby Pool, a lovely circular expanse of water, is beautiful at all seasons, but especially in a cold winter on a freezing day when the water birds collect in their hundreds in the ice-free patch of water just at the feet of the human visitors at the viewing point. Swans, geese, mallards, seagulls, wigeon, ruddy ducks (not so welcome as native varieties perhaps, but very pretty, nevertheless!) tufted ducks and teal, pochard, reed buntings and grebes can all be seen. The pool is a Site of Scientific Interest.

Newtown Linford: see previous walk. Marions Cottage (Tourist Bookshop and Information Point) is open at weekends.

The clock in the church tower was funded from proceeds of village pageant, *Lady Jane Returns*, given in the ruins of her house in Bradgate Park, 1951–2.

Martinshaw Woods has a main path accessible to wheelchairs. The trees screen the housing estate and the birdsong competes merrily with the traffic noise and the wood is delightful at all seasons.

INTO THE PARK
Groby   Newtown Linford   Bradgate

From Groby Church turn right to pass between the gravestone-ordered churchyard and a pretty, old slate-roofed house with picturesquely uneven walls, and walk down the tarmac strip with the church on your right. Pass under the thunderously noisy A50 dual carriageway and follow the strip as it swings left and goes up to the footpath sign. Turn right, through the big metal kissing gate and follow the well walked path straight across the open field until you meet the wooden kissing gate. Meet the quarry drive. Continue along the footpath ahead and go up the steps on your left to reach Groby Pool.

. **From Groby Pool** return to the road and turn right to pass Groby Pool car park and picnic site and nature trail on your right. Continue along the road to make a big sweeping curve downhill.

. Turn left at the footpath sign on your left just before the fork up to the A50 towards Leicester. Follow the wide tarmac drive which fishermen use to reach the lakes. At the end of the long narrow field, turn left, just before the ford where the track bends left. Walk with the stream on your right and cross the good footbridge over it.

3. Continue in the same direction across the field to the waymarked stil
by the isolated tree. There are two paths here. Turn left to take the on
which goes along the hedge. Sheet Hedges Wood lies ahead on the hil
Groby quarries can be seen encroaching on the woods over to your lef

4. Pass the fishing lakes on your left. Cross the double stile an
continue up towards Sheet Hedges. The path should go in a straigh
line up to the wood but there is a cleared and very well use
waymarked path to the gap in the corner of the field. Go uphill paralle
with the wood (and quarry) over to your left and meet the corner c
Sheet Hedges wood which juts out.

5. Walk uphill close to Sheet Hedges wood on your left. At the top c
the hill you have views of Charnwood ahead. Meet a good track (fror
Anstey and Cropston) and turn left along it.

6. Follow the northern boundary of Sheet Hedges. Go through the littl
projecting corner of the wood and follow the well used track. Cross th
stile which leads into the corner of a big field. (The path should g
diagonally across from this point, between Sheet Hedges wood on you
left and the hedge on your right, to a waymarker post in the far righ
hedge but the field is usually ploughed and most walkers follow th
headland round to the right as it is not much further.) Make for the marke
post and then continue close to the hedge on your right. (Old John an
the war memorial on the hill now come into view over to your right.)

7. Meet a wide gap in the hedge, where a farm track goes toward
Cork Hall farm on your right. The path should go across this track an
continue in the same direction and then go diagonally right in the ne
field, but once again this field is usually, illegally, ploughed and th
farmers' notices and waymark signs signs indicate that you should g
along the track towards the farm and then turn left into the field an
walk with the hedge on your right. (Decide for yourself which is easie
Aim for the waymark post in the hedge on your right, just before the bi
farm sheds.

8. Turn right and immediately left to follow a very unfriendly fenced o
path, with lots of awkward stiles and quite unnecessary barbed wire
passing the farmsheds on your right.

9. Join a wide drive which takes you down past Stone End and no 52
to meet Bradgate Road, Newtown Linford. Turn left and continue pa
the park entrance to reach Newtown Linford church.

At this point you can return without doing the next loop. The footpat
back to Groby is opposite the church, between the cafe and the Po
Office. The next section is the optional extra loop.

0. Continue along the road, towards the Bradgate Arms pub. Pass the Groby Lane junction. At the village pump, turn right and follow the footpath sign To Woodhouse Eaves. Pass house number 19 and cross the granite stile. Go up the lovely old wide green hollow-way. Cross the fence and continue uphill towards Tyburn Hill, the spinney on the hill beyond the high park wall. Go through the kissing gate in the top pointed corner of the field and turn right to follow the park wall back down to Newtown Linford.

This is a lovely downhill track. You can keep to the wide bridleway or follow the footpath which keeps close to the park wall on your right. Walk through the main car park and turn right at the road by the church. The return footpath to Groby is opposite the church.

1. **From Newtown Linford** take the footpath to Groby by following the narrow hedged footpath which goes from the bus stop between the cafe and the Post Office. Continue uphill in the next long and narrow paddock. (Do not feed the donkey!) Cross over the stile in the top left corner and meet the road on a dangerous bend.

2. Cross carefully to the gateway opposite and continue along the stony track to go through a farmgate at the end of the first field. (This is path J92, mentioned in the Items of Interest, where the proposed conveyor belt tunnel is to be built. If you parked at Groby Pool and wish to take short cut back you will be able to swing left at this point on the new proposed route. It should be indicated.)

3. To continue to Groby and Martinshaw Woods, follow the track which keeps close to the wood on the right and then cross a big pasture, moving slightly left of the wood to cross a cartbridge over the stream and continue diagonally up to the top left corner of the field, by a corner of Lady Hay Wood.

4. Cross the stile and continue close to Lady Hay Wood scrubland on your left and the quarry on your right. The houses of Markfield Road come into view ahead. Pass their garden fences and swing right on the track which takes you to the A50 road. We now take a big sweep through Martinshaw woods, to avoid this main road.

5. To cross the A50 road go to the traffic lights and wait! Then turn left to reach the footpath sign and turn right, by the roadbridge just before the huge warehouse and lorry park. A tarmac strip takes you uphill to meet the track into Martinshaw Woods.

6. Turn right to enter Martinshaw woods and keep to the main route which goes straight through the woods (due south). There are houses over to your left and a motorway ahead but you are in an oasis of peace and the wood is delightful.

17. At the far edge of the wood turn left to pass Groby Community College over to your right and follow the jitty path between houses 57/59 on Lawnwood Road. (This is a bus route.) Turn left and walk up the road. Pass Lawnwood shops and continue along Martinshaw Lane to meet the main road where you turn left to go downhill into Groby.

The Earl of Stamford pub stands at the foot of the hill. The church and the lovely old hall are to your left along Markfield Lane.

THE OLD MILL BY THE STREAM
Markfield **Ulverscroft Mill** **Newtown Linford** **8**
(Newtown Linford can be omitted if you start from Markfield)

Distance 5 miles (plus a litle extra if you include Newtown Linford).

How to get there Markfield lies north west of Leicester on the A50. Newtown Linford lies on the Anstey Lane route out of Leicester.

Starting points The walk can be started at either end. Both villages can be used as a refreshment stop half way round. In Markfield parking is available in the small carpark in Main Street on corner of Uplands Drive.
In Newtown Linford if you use the Bradgate car park, be back by dusk, when the gates shut.

Bus routes Both villages can be reached by bus. Markfield bus 117, 118, 119
Newtown Linford buses 121, 123, 73, 74, 76 and 123 run hourly. Ring Busline for details.

Refreshment Newtown Linford, the gateway to Bradgate park, provides all facilities
Markfield has shops and pubs.
(Do not expect tea at Blakeshay Farm. It is no longer the welcoming tea place we all knew and loved.)

The route An easy five miles, for those who can tackle stiles and hills. There are lots of pretty things to look at as you go, slowly, uphill. The rhododrendrons, much disliked by conservationists, because they do not support insect life, are nevertheless very pretty.
The views are of course spectacular. Old John and the war memorial can be clearly seen and Charnwood really does look like a forest in these quiet hidden places! (See it in autumn when the leaves of the forest are just turning to various shades of gold.)

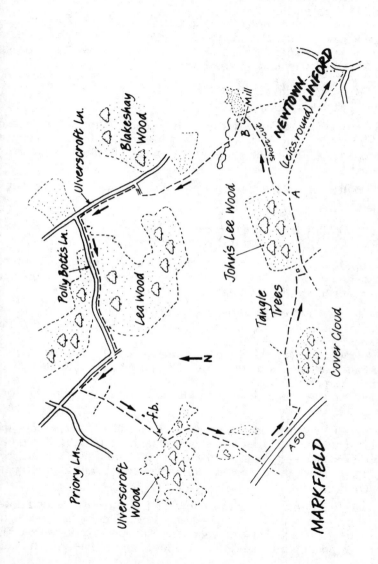

Items of interest

Main Street, Markfield, has an interesting variety of domestic architecture, including the big Congregational Chapel, established in 1852 and the Miners' Welfare Hall. (The name tells you something of Markfield's past history!)

If you have time and energy to explore Markfield, go up to see the old quarry (but keep a careful eye on any children with you!) The view from the trig. point is spectacular, a marvellous place to view Charnwood. The Altar Rocks are up on the old A50.

Johns Lee Wood has a scout camp

Ulverscroft Mill is now in ruins.

Lea Cottage and Stoneywell Cottage designed by Ernest Gimson and built for the Gimson family at the turn of the century. Gimson was part of the Design in Industry movement, much influenced by William Morris.

Polly Bott's Lane. Did a Mrs Polly Bott really live here? Who was she?

THE OLD MILL BY THE STREAM
Markfield   Ulverscroft Mill   Newtown Linford

1. From Markfield walk up Main Street, passing the Red Lion pub on your left and continue to the top of the road. Take the right fork and turn right when you meet the Leicester Road.

2. Walk downhill for a short distance. Pass the bus shelter on your left and turn left at the Leicestershire Round footpath sign. A tarmac strip path leads you between fences.
Here you have fine views of Charnwood. The war memorial in Bradgate park stands on the hill ahead with Tyburn Hill to the right of it, and the masts at Copt Oak to the left
Follow the path which leads you through the tunnel under the A50. Turn right.

3. Cross the waymarked Leicestershire Round stile and walk along the wooded sloping bank with the A50 road up on your right. This pretty path joins the road verge for the next 100 yards. (It is not far, but enough to make you appreciate the peace and quiet of the footpath route!)

4. Swing left at the signpost to follow the Leicestershire Round down the slope. In the field follow the barbed wire fencing on your right Cross the waymarked stile on your right. You now keep in line with the war memorial in Bradgate Park, straight ahead of you, making you

way gradually uphill to meet the corner of Cover Cloud wood on your right.

5. Keep close to the edge of the wood and keep in the same direction close to the hedge on your right. (There is nasty barbed wire on both sides, so take care while you admire the beautiful wooded hilly countryside all around.) Cross the stile on your right and turn left to Tangle Trees farm, the white farmhouse ahead.

6. Move to the right hand corner of the field and cross the stile to pass Tangle Trees farm on your left. Pass the old barn and cross the track from the scout camp car park. Continue close to Johns Lee Wood on your left. Follow the Leicestershire Round signs until you reach the corner of the wood The waymark signs now change to simple arrows.

7. (A) Here the Leicestershire Round leaves our track. If you wish to go into Newtown Linford, continue following the Leicestershire Round waymark signs to reach the road. Turn left and then right to reach the centre of Newtown Linford. Bradgate park entrance is on your left just beyond the church. Explore the delights of the village! Have tea and coffee or other drinks and food before you return to point (B) at Ulverscroft Mill to continue the walk.

From Newtown Linford to point (B) walk along the road, passing the church on your right. Ignore the turn to Markfield on your left. Turn left at the footpath sign opposite the Johnscliffe Hotel, down a track between houses.
Cross the stile into a narrow neck of a field between hedge and stream. The path now continues over fields, with trees on your left. The tree-lined little River Lin bends away from you as you go straight across the field. Continue in the same direction until you meet the Sharpley Hill-Markfield green lane. Turn left to pass the old Ulverscroft Mill on your right. Cross the stile by the gate and swing sharp right, to go uphill keeping close to the fence of the tall, old mill in its gloomy shaded dell down on your right.(B)

8. (A) If you do not wish to go into Newtown Linford, take the short cut to point (B) by following the wood round to your left for a short distance. Turn right immediately after passing through the field corner. Walk downhill close to the hedge on your right. The war memorial lies straight ahead on the hill.

Continue steeply downhill, crossing several stiles. When you meet the stream look for the old Ulverscroft Mill ahead, in the little hollow on your left. Here our path turns left, to keep the old mill, down on our right. (B)

9. **Both routes continue from point (B)**. Cross the stile into an open meadow field, with sloping ridge and furrows. (The signpost To Ulverscroft is hidden in the hedge.) Move diagonally left to the far corner of the field. Cross the good footbridge with handrail. Walk close to the stream. Ignore the ford and continue close to the stream on your left.

The well trodden path goes uphill in the next field, moving slightly right. Cross the high footstool fence and continue in the same direction across the long meadow which slopes up to the far right corner.

10. Cross the rough old fence with stones for footstools and follow the old green lane track. The track takes a sharp right turn and meets the road from Newtown Linford, near the drive to Blakeshay Farm.

11. Turn left and follow the road for a quarter of a mile. Turn left again down Polly Botts Lane, signposted to Chitterman Hills. Follow this lovely wooded road uphill between Lea Wood and Stoneywell Wood. The road bends sharp right, passing private drives to Lea Wood and Chitterman Hill Farm on your left. Continue uphill to pass Lea Cottage on your right.

12. Turn left at the signpost by the telegraph pole opposite the welcoming seat near the top of the hill. Walk downhill (at last!) close to the wall and hedge on your right.

Markfield church lies ahead, on the hill. Keep in this direction going downhill, over a series of rather poor stiles and crossing the drive to Chitterman Hill Farm. You will have a wood on your right at first, then a hedge on your left. Ahead lies Ulverscroft Wood.

13. Ignore the gate in the bottom corner of the field and take the narrow hedged green path just to the right of it. This leads you round the edge of Ulverscroft Wood on your right. (The nasty barbed wire is to be avoided as unfriendly. Please refer any damage to clothing to the farmer concerned!) Continue along the pretty green tunnel of trees and keep in the same direction along the wide track Cross the drive from Home Farm. (Shetland ponies are often in the fields to your left.)

14. The noisy main A50 road lies ahead. The wide track, goes gradually uphill, over a fine stone bridge. Cross the fence and go up revetted steps to the bank of the road. At this point you can see the tunnel passage under the A50 which returns you to Markfield.

To reach the centre of Markfield village, turn right at the Leicester road and go uphill. Turn left and go downhill to the carpark where you started.

15. If you started from Newtown Linford turn left before the tunnel and follow parags 3–7.

From this happy combination of public and private action those who know the surroundings of Woodhouse Eaves may feel assured that they may look forward to the maintenance of what they have grown to value in the past.
Paget and Irvine, County Books Leicestershire p 176

Distance A circuit of about 5 miles if you start from the car park in Woodhouse Eaves. Slightly less if you start from Maplewell Road.
There is a possible short cut at Broombriggs, but it cuts out one of the highlights of the walk. The more direct route keeps to the flat land and goes straight to Beacon Hill.
The walk could be divided into two and enjoyed on two separate days.

Starting points Woodhouse Eaves has a car park and toilets in the recreation ground on Main Street, opposite the impressive red brick Wesleyan methodist chapel.
Beacon Hill carparks make an alternative start. The lower car park is on Breakback Road, Woodhouse Eaves. The upper one is on the B591, near the top of the hill.

How to get there Woodhouse Eaves is on the B591 and well signposted from Anstey, Rothley, Quorn or Nanpantan.

Bus routes: Regular bus service (hourly) to Woodhouse Eaves from Leicester or Loughborough.

Refreshment Woodhouse Eaves has three pubs (the Curzon Arms, the Pear Tree Inn and Ye Olde Bulls Head), all serving food.

The route Mainly permissive paths through one of the most scenic parts of Charnwood Forest, across Broombriggs and Beacon Hill. For very short walks you could do each circuit separately. Both circuits are well used and well waymarked There are many possible routes over both sites. You can choose whichever suits your style and the time available. The views from the top are magnificent

Items of interest Woodhouse Eaves makes an interesting start to a walk. There are lots of attractive slate roofed buildings, an Enclosure church built over a rock cave, and a beautiful round modern chapel (which often serves teas and refreshments. Look out for the welcoming signs!)

Broombriggs farm trail gives plenty of interesting information about farming, on noticeboards along the route.

Beacon Hill, one of the highest points in Leicestershire, was once a

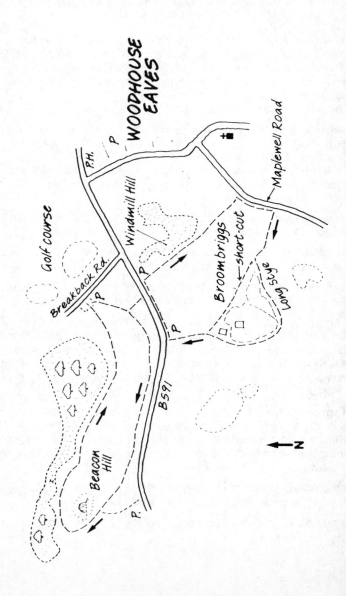

Bronze Age hill fort. It is now open access country (bought by Leicestershire County council in 1947 when the Beaumanor estate was sold) and there are many possible paths down from the top. Roman coins were found at the foot of the hill.

The windmill on Windmill Hill stood as an impressive landmark until it was destroyed by fire in 1945. Only the brick base now remains. The hill was bought by the LCC when the Beaumanor estate was sold.

'FOR QUIET PUBLIC ENJOYMENT'
Woodhouse Eaves   Broombriggs   Beacon Hill

1. **From Maplewell Road, Woodhouse Eaves**, take the wide grassy path beside house number 100. Turn left through the bridle gate and then immediately right to walk on the well used path, close to the hedge on your right. Pass, over to your left, the wooded knoll of Round Stye spinney, and walk towards Long Stye spinney, the wood which goes up the hill ahead to your left.

2. When you reach the foot of Long Stye spinney the farm trail route goes left, steeply uphill. (But you can if you wish take a short cut to Beacon Hill by continuing straight ahead, keeping to the hedge on your right. If you choose this route you miss the hills and the most beautiful views. In the last field before the road pass Broombriggs House in the trees over to your left. Follow the telegraph lines diagonally left to reach the drive from the House, paragraph 8.)

3. For the farm trail route round Broombriggs, go steeply uphill close to the stone wall of Long Stye wood on your right. The view from the top is worth the climb! You can look back to Windmill Hill and beyond to Quorn and the Soar Valley.

4. Go through the little triangular walled enclosure into the picnic site field, where you have views over the other side of the hill, eastwards over to Copt Oak and Ulverscroft.

5. At the end of Long Stye spinney keep in the same direction and cross the stile, beyond the farm gates. Move towards the wall over to your left, but do not cross it. (Beyond the field wall, lies the farm of Upper Broombriggs).

6. Go uphill, with the wall on your left, to the little clump of trees, (a walled enclosure of holly and beech, beside a waymarked seat), in the top left corner of the field. Cross the stile and continue gradually uphill close to the enclosure wall on your left. You are now at the top of Broombriggs Hill, 200 metres above sea level, with Broombriggs

House down to your right.

7. Keep close to the fenced off bracken and gorse and make a big semicircular sweep around Broombriggs House, going gradually downhill with the plantation wall on your left. Continue on the wide fenced-off grass sward and meet the wide, walled drive from Broombriggs House.

8. Continue down the drive to meet Beacon Road (B591). (Woodhouse Eaves lies to your right.) Cross carefully and keep in the same direction, through the belt of woodland.
Meet the main track up to Beacon Hill. Turn left and walk uphill to the highest point.

9. From the top of Beacon Hill take any path downhill towards Woodhouse Eaves.
If you leave the main track you can take your bearing from the toposcope and aim straight for Woodhouse Eaves, going steeply downhill through the bracken to meet the main drive, which leads into Lower Beacon car park.
(The firm metalled track encircles the hill. You can follow it all the way round, to go back down to Woodhouse Eaves, passing the rocky outcrop of the Devil's Profile, on your right, then going downhill directly to Beacon Hill lower car park, where there are toilets and ice creams etc.)

10. For Woodhouse Eaves, turn right, just before you reach the car park. Follow the path which leads back to Beacon Road. (B591) (Ye Olde Bulls Head is along Beacon Road to your left.) Windmill Hill lies ahead. Cross over Beacon Road to reach the little car park, a short way down the road and follow the waymarked path to Windmill Hill.

11. Pass Windmill Hill on your left. (If you wish to climb to the top to see the base of the old windmill, turn left as you enter the trees. From the summit you can follow the well walked path and return to this track a little further on.)
The track leads through the woodland below the hill and joins Mill Road. Turn left at Maplewell Road and walk downhill into Woodhouse Eaves.

'Directions to tourists:
Never fail therefore when desirous of seeing plantations or enclosed grounds to procure the occupier's permission to ramble about them. A note, addressed to the owner of the estate, a few days previously, may save the party from a summary dismissal by the keeper.'
Companion to Charnwood Forest   1858

Distance 5 miles. 2½ hours gentle walking but allow time for loitering in the woods and for stopping to admire the views.

Starting point Ratby has a small public car park park by the library, opposite the primary school on the main road.

How to get there Ratby is 5 miles northwest of Leicester, just north of Kirby Muxloe, between Desford and Groby and can be approached from the A50 or the A47,

Bus routes 113, 114, 217, 218. Ring Busline for details.

Refreshment Various pubs and a fish bar. The Bulls Head and the Plough Inn both serve food.

The route 5 miles easy walking through woods and pasture. Good tracks, a small stretch of main road and a short stretch of country road (less noisy but just as dangerous). Some bridleways which get muddy in wet weather. Good views

Items of interest
Ratby lies between Charnwood and the ancient Royal Forest of Leicester. The older parts of the village are clustered round the Norman church. Stamford Street has interesting Victorian terraced houses and Edwardian villas dated 1896, 1903 and 1906. Ratby once had a thriving framework knitting industry, and nearby quarrying and coalmining.

Martinshaw Woods are managed by Woodland Trust and you are welcome to use any paths and to explore as you wish. The notice boards indicate the main tracks through the wood and give a brief indication of the history and wildlife to be found. It was part of the deer park belonging to the de Ferrars family in the 13th century.
Toot Hills is a prominent outcrop of Pre-Cambrian rocks about 500 million years old. Stone was once quarried here and there are flooded pits on the western side. Trees were coppiced until 1920s when large scale felling took place. The Forestry Commission replanted trees in 1950–4. The M1 motorway, constructed in 1963, cut through the

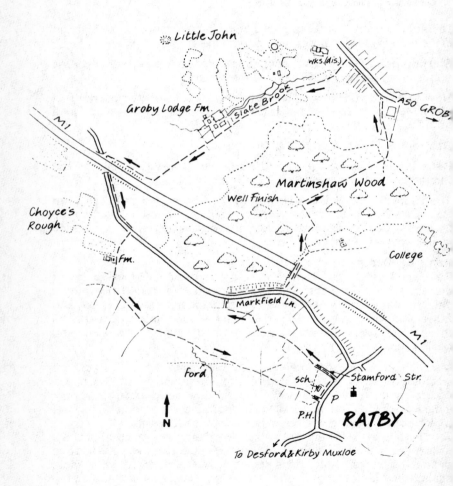

woods. Near the crossroad of tracks at Well Finish there is an interesting boggy area for flowers and moss and willow herbs. The flooded pits are favourite haunts of frogs and newts.

Stop for as long as you like, picnic, count 36 varieties of trees, flowers and birds and then continue the walk. Our route goes on wide main tracks through the heart of the wood, emerging at Groby on the A50.

Grey Lodge has a most beautiful drive, with slate walls. It follows the Slate Brook on your right and passes two large and very beautiful houses in their own grounds The pool has swans and ducks. The gardens are a mass of snowdrops in March and are lovely at all seasons.

Bondman Hays was an early clearing in the forest. It was only ever a small hamlet.

OUR WOODLAND TRUST
Ratby   Martinshaw   Slate Brook   Choyce's Rough

From Ratby walk up the main street, with the church and Church Lane over to your right.

1. Turn left along Stamford Street. Go straight ahead through the kissing gate at the end of the road and follow the fenced off path down to the field corner. Martinshaw Woods stand rather gloomily ahead and there are other woods on the hills all around.

2. Cross the series of waymarked fences with big stone footstools. Keep parallel with telegraph poles over to your left, aiming for the left end of the neat row of suburban ribbon development houses edging Martinshaw Wood.

3. At a bend in the hedge cross the stile into a hedged lane and meet the Markfield Road. We cannot cross straight through the woods because of the motorway which bisects it. Turn right along the road. (Follow the service road, to avoid the worst of the traffic perils.)

4. When the service road ends (opposite the bus terminus shelter) turn left into the woods. Ignore the first gate, which only leads into the southern section of the wood but continue along the concrete drive to cross the motorway.

5. From the motorway bridge, swing left to enter the woods (ignoring the footpath which forks right and goes outside the woods, to Groby)

6. Go down the concrete slope into the woods then take the first (little)

path on your right. This path winds gradually uphill to meet a main path. Turn left to follow this wide, edged track until you meet a well defined crossroads at a high point in the centre of the wood (Well Finish crossroads).

7. Turn right at Well Finish crossroads and follow the straight track to the end of the wood. (A distant bungalow may be glimpsed at the far end.) Pass a rustic bridge fencing and a path to your right and continue towards the bungalow. Two further rustic fence bridges lie ahead, just before the bungalow. Turn left at the second and follow the edged path, (with houses over to your right) to go through the wooden gateway.

8. Join the narrow path by the fencing of the house gardens. Swing left and go downhill, over scrubby ground passing the big brick warehouses on your right.

9. Turn left along the A50 Markfield Road, Groby. Pass the traffic lights and continue uphill for 100 paces (There is a bus shelter over to your right.) Turn left at the bridleway, signposted to Grey Lodge. The drive follows the meandering stream, with Martinshaw up on your left.

10. Fork left at the drive to Grey Lodge. Pass the pool on your right. The metalled drive and the slate walls end near the farm buildings on your right. Continue on the farm track (often muddy). On the Motorway ahead the cars and lorries look like Dinky toys.

11. At the motorway turn right for two fields. (The stiles are rather high but the gates will usually open.) Meet the road on your left and go downhill under the motorway. (This is a country road but the traffic tries to rival the Motorway traffic, so beware!)

12. Ignore the first footpath on your right (to Whittington Rough) and follow the road as it bends left.

13. Turn right at Cow Lane. Fork left on the bridleway to pass the house on your right and follow the tree-lined farm track to reach the stream.

14. Where the main drive swings right we turn left on the footpath This follows a raised prettily wooded embankment with a stream on the left and boggy areas down to the right. Pass a scrubby bit of woodland then cross the solid handrailed footbridge. Continue beside the stream on your right.

15. The squat tower of Ratby church comes into view ahead. Keep in this direction. In the third field the stream moves away from you and you cut off the wet corner of field to your right. Go gradually uphill, still

in the same direction, to meet at the top of the hill the old road which comes in on your right over the ford.

16 Continue along the old road, ignoring footpaths on your left (which lead to Stamford Street). Aim straight for Ratby church tower and go downhill all the way to the main road, passing the Plough Inn on Burroughs Road. The Bulls Head is to your right, and the school and war memorial on your left. The library car park and the church are uphill to your left.

A MEDIEVAL BYPASS
Ratby   Old Hays   Holywell

11

A board sticks up to notice 'no road here'.
John Clare, The Mores.

Distance 4 miles

Starting point Ratby. Car parks in village street

How to get there Ratby is 5 miles northwest of Leicester, just north of Kirby Muxloe, between Desford and Groby and can be approached from the A50 or the A47.

Bus routes 113 114 217 218. Ring Busline.

Refreshment Various pubs: The Bulls Head and The Plough both serve food.

The route: 4 miles easy walking on tracks in gently hilly country, through short patches of woodland. Much of our way is on the old track of a medieval bypass which goes round the edge of the Old Hays deer park. We skirt the boundary of the deer park which was itself created on the site of an Iron Age enclosure.
Some of these bridleways get muddy in wet weather.
There are good views in this rolling countryside.

Items of interest
Ratby lies between Charnwood and the ancient Royal Forest of Leicester. It has an interesting mix of old village clustered round Norman church and industrial remains of a once thriving framework knitting industry, and nearby quarrying and coalmining.
There used to be a Crow Pie carnival in Ratby. It is better known now for Geary's Rearsby loaves, made here.

Burrough Park, once a deer park, was part of Whitwick manor and

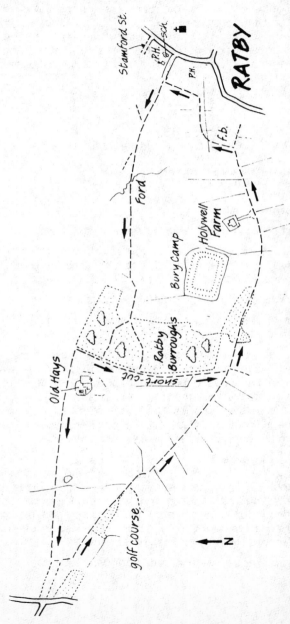

owned by Elizabeth Buchan in 1270. By about 1312 it became part of Groby Manor. The park was situated on the Iron Age enclosure of Bury Camp, using its ramparts as a boundary for the deer. It is now on private land. One corner of the boundary mound is just visible from the track near Holywell if you stop and look up in the right direction.

Ratby Burroughs Wood was recently used for war games, which deterred many walkers, but the wood has now been purchased by the Woodland Trust and should soon be waymarked.

Old Hays a 13th century moated farmhouse. The many footpaths which once crossed close to it have now been diverted round the edge of the field, so you only get a distant view. But you can see signs on the ground of the ancient paths which led to the farmhouse. Its name indicates that it was an ancient enclosure from the forest. (It was in fact recorded as an assart of the wasteland in 1250.) The land, once owned by Leicester Abbey was bought by Francis Cave (in the 1530s) at the time of the Dissolution of the Abbeys. It was later bought by the Sacheverels, whose tombs are in Ratby church. In 1789 it was bought by the Earls of Stamford who sold it in 1929.

The golf course, with its new tracks and ponds and tree planting, is a recent addition.

A MEDIEVAL BYPASS
Ratby   Old Hays   Holywell

1. **From Ratby** main street near the war memorial, turn along Burroughs Road and pass the Plough Inn on your right. Go gradually uphill on the good track. (Over to your right the conifer trees of Martinshaw Woods beyond a line of houses. The squat tower of Ratby church behind.) Go downhill to cross the ford and footbridge then uphill again, with fine views (and an occasional brief glimpse of the motorway over to your right).

2. As you approach the corner of Ratby Burroughs wood the tree-lined drive bends left and right. Look out for a stile on your right, opposite a small brick building on your left. (We now take a footpath to cut a corner of the lane. If you prefer to keep on the lane, turn right at the next crossroads of paths and pass Old Hays as in paragraph 4.)

3. Cross the stile and, with your back to the little brick building, cut across the field, walking from Ratby Burroughs wood to a sparser wood ahead. (Note Ratby church tower through the gap. Keep walking away from it.) Cross the stile about half way along the wood ahead. The trees are widely spaced here and the various tracks may look a bit

confusing, but just keep in the same general direction on any good path, with the main body of thicker wood on your right and you will come to the boundary wire of the wood. You should emerge at the boundary directly opposite the big farmhouse of Old Hays. Cross the stile.

4. Turn right and follow the edge of the wood, passing Old Hays farm in the middle of the field on your left. At the end of the wood we need to turn left to go along the top hedge of the field but to reach it you will need to go though a handgate in the top right corner, walk a few paces and then turn left. Follow the bridleway, close to the hedge on your right, with Old Hays now down to your left in the middle of the field.

5. Keep close to the hedge on your right, ignoring any paths off it. Follow a sunken track which leads towards Thornton. (We do not go all the way to Thornton.) The track goes downhill to cross the stream and then uphill as a very pretty treelined lane The golf course can be seen ahead. Continue up the hedged track (often muddy) with the golf course beyond the hedge on the left.

6. Turn sharp left when you meet the main track, (which goes straight on to Thornton). Follow the bridleway which begins as a very beautiful tree-lined track with the golf course now on your left. Pass Crow Wood on your right. Ignore paths to right and left and keep on the tree-lined track. Pass various lakes and a couple of big houses up on the right. The wood ahead is Ratby Burroughs

7. When you meet the wood swing right and then left to keep in the same direction. Move to the right of the ditch and walk with it on your left (and Ratby Burroughs beyond it.)

8. Go through the handgate into the small conifer wood and follow the wide track. (When the gravel ends it may be muudy here!) Continue close to the stream on your left and continue in the same direction to pass Holywell Farm. (This is the place to start looking up to the hill on your left, to see the site of the Iron Age encampment on the high ground beyond the hedge on your left It stands on private ground. We have to be content with just a glimpse of a small corner of the mound!)

9. Ratby church tower comes into view ahead. Descend the bank to join the track from Holywell farm. (To avoid the stiles in the next section, you can continue along this drive all the way to the road and then turn left to walk along the road into Ratby.)

10. Turn left to leave the track halfway along the second field. Cross the waymarked footbridge by a big grassy semicircle and continue

straight up the field. Go over the stile and continue diagonally right to cut off a little field corner to cross a second stile. Then head straight for Ratby church tower. Go under the telegraph lines towards a big farm but move to the left hedge to cross the stile. Cross the farm track and follow the fenced off path to walk with the track on your left. (These last three stiles feel very unfriendly at the end of a walk!)

11. Meet the lane and turn right to go downhill past the Plough Inn.

12. Turn left at the road and go uphill to reach the library car park. The church is a bit further on along the road on your right.

ANCIENT CLEARINGS IN THE FOREST   **12**
Thornton   Whittington   Bondman Hays

If the hills were planted and other parts enclosed it would be a wonderful ornament to the country.
Agricultural report for Leicestershire   1794

Distance 5 miles

Starting point Thornton, near the church.

How to get there Thornton lies south of Markfield and can be reached from the A50.

Bus routes Thornton is on a regular bus route.

Refreshment The Bulls Head and The Plasterers Arms provide refreshment.

Parking (You could ask if you could park in the pub yards if you are eating their food.)
There is a convenient Community Hall car park, which can be used if there is no sports field function. Otherwise use roadside parking, with discretion.
Car parks by the reservoir are for anglers but there are small laybyes by the reservoir road.

The route From the high ground of Thornton you have lovely views of the reservoir. The surrounding countryside is hilly and the start of the walk, along the well marked Leicestershire Round, is quite steep. (The gentle stroll around the beautiful reservoir might make a tempting alternative for less strong walkers. But note that in the fishing season walkers are not welcomed there by anglers!)
We leave the Leicestershire Round to walk beside a stream and then

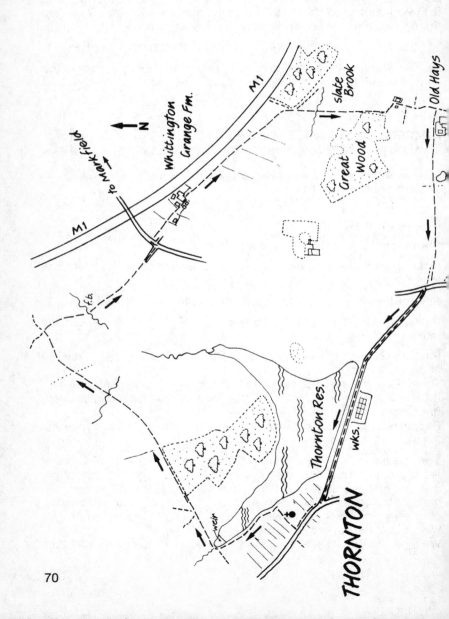

go up to walk beside the motorway. It is a great pity that this section of the walk is spoilt by proximity with the M1. There is little to commend the short stretch from Whittington Grange to Whittington Rough but it isn't far to the quiet of the valley and the wood. We have a lovely finish by woodland on old tracks, where the path is well waymarked and very pleasant, going though what seems to be an ancient hollow way with remains of old walls and ditches. This is the old deer park boundary of Old Hays and the parish boundary with Bagworth. We follow the road into Thornton over the reservoir dam.

Items of interest Thornton township dates from 1086. The church (1189) is worth a visit. (Keys from the shop on the corner during shop opening times.)

Thornton reservoir was constructed in 1853.

Bondman Hays was an early clearing of the forest.

Whittington was once an early settlement but the deserted village has lost its former glory and is now just a name on a map.

Whittington Rough is a wood used as a camping site for naturists.

ANCIENT CLEARINGS IN THE FOREST
Thornton   Whittington   Bondman Hays

1. **From Thornton** walk down Church Lane. Pass the lych gate with the church over to your right. Go steeply downhill on a good path to reach the reservoir track. Turn left to walk round beside the water, admiring the views. A path from the Community Centre hall and school comes down from your left)

2. Swing round the narrow end of the reservoir. Follow Leicestershire Round waymark signs, leaving the reservoir and making for the wood on the hill. Keep close to the hedge on your left. Ignore the first waymarked stile on your left but cross the second, and continue steeply uphill with the hedge now on your right. The top of the hill is a good place to stop and look around you (old coalfields to the back of you and Markfield and the rocks of Charnwood ahead).

3. Continue towards Markfield church spire, downhill with the hedge on your right at first and then go through the jutting out corner to walk with it on your left, (in a field with telegraph poles). Go downhill to cross the stile by a (muddy) gateway over the stream/ditch.

4. Continue uphill to pass a lone telegraph pole in the next, open field, keeping exactly in line with the hedge you have left. Cross the good

slate footplank and big stones at the parish boundary hedge at the top of the hill. The M1 is visible and audible now

5. Go steeply downhill through a little spinney to reach the stream. Cross the good footplank and then turn sharp right, (leaving the Leicestershire Round).

6. Keep close to the stream hedge on your right. A well trodden path leads you over a stile and across two substantial handrailed bridges which take you over the boggy junction of two streams.

7. Go uphill from the second bridge across the open field. (Good views from the top of the hill!) Continue to the road

8. Go slightly left to cross the road. Follow the footpath which begins as the drive to Whittington Grange. Pass the house and stables and the bungalow and farmbuildings. Continue on the (muddy) farm track, keeping in the same direction, parallel with and close to the M1. There are no waymarks and no landmarks in this stony field. A few old trees remain to mark old hedge lines

9. Meet and walk with a hedge on your left and go downhill in the same direction, with the hedge now on your right to meet Whittington Rough. (A track to the camp in the woods comes down over the motorway to your left.)

10. Cross the stile in the corner of the field to the right of the woods. Turn right and walk uphill close to the hedge on your right. Cross the railed footbridge and stile over the Slate Brook and continue uphill. The wood over to your right is Great Wood. At the end of the field you walk close to the wood.

11. Cross the waymarked stile at the end of Great Wood and go diagonally towards the right hand side of the house, with sheds and garages to your right. Cross the waymarked stile by the gate, pass sheds and follow the track round to the right, passing a ruined house (being demolished) on your left. Continue on the fenced-off path, going downhill. Keep in this direction close to a hedge on your left.

12. In the far corner of the field cross the stile to continue straight ahead across an open field (usually ploughed, but with a reinstated footpath). The farm ahead is Old Hays

13. When you reach the field with the farm in it, turn right and follow the fenced-off field edge. Keep the hedge on your right all the way to the road.

14. The road to Thornton is signposted straight ahead. Go downhill

along this road to cross the reservoir dam and go uphill to the road junction. Turn right to The Bulls Head, the church, shops and bus stops and The Plasterers Arms.

OVER BUCK HILL TO THE DEVIL'S PROFILE
The Outwoods   Permissive Paths
Deans Lane

13

Their pointed crags have all the characteristics of a mountain range, while the mossy turf enables one to enjoy a most luxurious ramble among them (The Hanging Stone or Pocket Gate Rocks).
The Companion to Charnwood Forest 1858 (reprinted by Orchard Press)

Distance $3\frac{1}{2}$ miles
If you start from Wodhouse Eaves add on a mile each way

Starting points Woodhouse Eaves or the Outwoods car park

How to get there to reach the Outwoods from Woodhouse Eaves by car, turn off the B591 and follow Breakback Road, signposted to Nanpantan. There is some roadside carparking in laybyes on Breakback Road and a small car park in the centre of the Outwoods, on your right (but note that this closes at dusk). Slow down and signal clearly: traffic goes fast on these straight roads through the forest.

Bus routes Regular buses to Woodhouse Eaves. Alight at Ye Old Bulls Head and walk along Brook Lane to reach the Deans Lane crossroads and The Outwoods

Refreshment Woodhouse Eaves has lots of good eating places and shops which sell food. If you take a picnic, Beacon Hill makes a good viewing stop (with nearby ice cream stalls).

The route
Through woodland then over hilly and rocky land with fine views.
The Buck Hill route requires your sensible footwear! If you prefer to avoid the steep climb over Buck Hill you can turn left along the road and take the next entrance on your right, near Charnwood Hall.)
A gradual descent on well kept paths gives a lovely walk along the secluded valley of the Woodbrook, with views of the impressive Nanpantan Hall. A stiffish climb through open woodland up to Beacon Hill.

Items of interest
The Outwoods a gift from the Moss family of Loughborough. There are

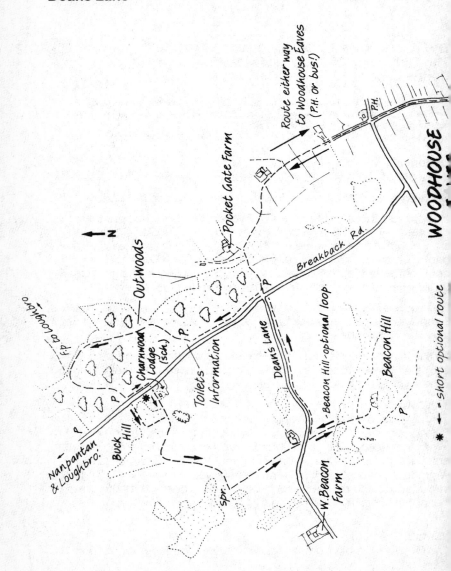

...e kissing gate at the start of the permissive path from Deans Lane.

many permissive paths through the mile long woods. The central spine of the woods is made up of impressive volcanic rocks. There are interesting exotic birds in the car park cottage garden and notice boards describe interesting features of wildlife in the woods.

Buck Hill: the permissive route over this fine rocky volcanic outcrop was recently donated by a member of the Paget family of Nanpantan Hall, when she inherited the land. The craggy rocks give a marvellous viewing point. From the top of Buck Hill you can look over the tall trees and admire the views all round you (Nanpantan Hall, Longcliffe Hill, Beacon Hill, Loughborough and the whole valley beyond).

Beacon Hill, the second highest hill in Leicestershire (248 m) with sharply pointed creamy white volcanic rocks. A favourite beauty spot with outstanding views. There is evidence that it was once a late Bronze Age Hill Fort. The Devils Profile can be detected as an outline of rocks by those with a good visual imagination

Hangingstone rock and golf course. The rocks were a favourite picnic spot for Leicestershire people in the early part of this century. It was thought that they would remain permanently accessible to the public Paget and Irvine wrote, (in The County Books: Leicestershire, p 176) *The future of the Hanging Rocks which adjoin the Beacon enclosure on the east, has also been assured by the action of certain members of Charnwood Golf Club, who have for many years been allowed by successive owners of Beaumanor to play on this ground at a nominal rental. They have now bought the area, with the intention of giving to members of the public the same degree of access as has been customary in the past, while preserving its amenities and its character as a golf course.*
From this happy combination of public and private action those who know the surroundings of Woodhouse Eaves may feel assured that they may look forward to the maintenance of what they have grown to value in the past.
Unhappily the present owners of the golf course have not fulfilled this promise and access is denied.

West Beacon Farm has modern windmills for energy conservation.

OVER BUCK HILL TO THE DEVIL'S PROFILE
The Outwoods   Permissive Paths   Deans Lane

From Woodhouse Eaves carpark or bus stop, walk away from the church, The Forest Rock and The Pear Tree to reach Ye Olde Bulls Head at the other end of the village. Cross the road and continue along

...ture conifer woods on the way to Buck Hill.

Brook Lane, passing Hangingstone farm on your right and the edge of the golf course on your left. The lane becomes a track which swings left to meet the road, opposite Deans Lane. Turn right for about 70 paces and enter the Outwoods. Walk parallel with the road on your left until you reach the Outwoods carpark and information board.

1. **From The Outwoods car park** and information board pass behind the toilet block to make your way across the wood. There are many little paths. You can choose whichever you fancy. Keep moving away from the road in the same general direction. You will need to cross a main path which goes along the length of the wood. Aim for the hilly craggy ridge of rocks which form the spine of the Outwoods and make your way down to the main track on the far boundary.

2. Turn left along the main track, with the wall on your right. Keep in this direction, passing impressive rocks on your left. The track bends sharp left by a seat and information board.

3. Follow this path (inside the wood, with Jubilee Wood on your right).

4. Meet the Nanpantan to Woodhouse Eaves road and cross over to the notice board near Buck Hill Lodge. The notice board informs you of the permissive path and asks you to keep dogs on leads. Waymark signs, stiles and kissing gates lead you over the route.
(Note that the easier route, avoiding Buck Hill, is to your left along the road. You can avoid the steep climb by turning right, near Charnwood Hall. Continue from paragraph 7.)

5. The path to Buck Hill begins by going uphill, (with a wall on your left, and Buck Hill Lodge over to your right) to enter a little circle of walled woodland. The path continues close to the wall on the left. Pass two open fields over to your left and emerge into the corner of the second field, where you walk with the fence on your right. (Nanpantan Hall is over to your right, across the valley.) Cross the corner of this field, where the fence meets a wall. The path is narrow, rocky and steep as it winds round and up to reach the peak of Buck Hill.

6. Continue along the ridge to another belt of woodland. The land slopes steeply down to the stream on your right. The woodland track leads you gently down. When you meet the boundary wall, keep it on your right and follow it round a sharp turn right.

7. Here the easier path from Charnwood Hall comes in from your left and both paths go downhill along a wide grassy track through bracken, and through the woodland which borders the stream.

8. A gap in the wall leads you across a footbridge, where you turn left.

e impressive Nanpantan Hall and volcanic diorite rocks of Charnwood.

Looking into the secluded Woodbrook valley from the slopes of Buck Hill.

9. Walk with the stream on your left along the valley through two big meadows. Just before the end of the third field, turn left, ford the stream and make your way uphill with an old wall on your right. (You may hear the gentle swishing of the electric windmills of West Beacon farm over to your right as you toil up the hill.)

10. At the end of the woodland track, winding gently uphill, go through the kissing gate and meet Deans Lane. Here we turn left.
(But to make a short extension to reach Beacon Hill, go through the metal gate opposite and follow the path to Beacon Hill. Pass the end of the Rippin Memorial path on your right and then turn left through the wall gap. Straight ahead of you is a ridge of jagged rocks and beyond them, through another little gap in the wall, the main gravel path round the hill. The outcrop of rocks which form the 'Devil's profile', come into view to your left. Uphill to the right of them is the Triangulation point, and to the right of this the toposcope which identifies for you the places all around you which can be seen from here. Return by the same route to Deans Lane.)

12 Go down Deans Lane, passing Beacon Hill and the Devils Profile up to your right and Beacon Cottage and Blackbirds Nest on your left.

13. At the crossroads with the Nanpantan-Woodhouse road turn left to walk through the Outwoods to the car park or to return to Woodhouse Eaves, continue along the track opposite Deans Lane and swing right to return by the route you came on, past Hangingtone farm into Brook Lane, emerging at Ye Olde Bulls Head.

OUT TO THE OUTWOODS, THE POCKET GATE WAY **14**
Loughborough   The Outwoods

I would direct the tourist to the Hangingstone Rock
An Illustrated Handbook to the Charnwood Forest   1857 (anon)

Distance $3\frac{1}{2}$ miles

Starting points The car park in the Outwoods or Loughborough (at the end of Moat Road, near the junction of Valley Road, Belvoir Drive and Beacon Road)

How to get there Loughborough is north of Leicester. The Outwoods lie between Nanpantan and Woodhouse Eaves, on Breakback Road.

Bus routes To Loughborough or to Woodhouse Eaves. (The walk from Woodhouse Eaves adds a mile each way.) Barton, Kinch, Midland Fox

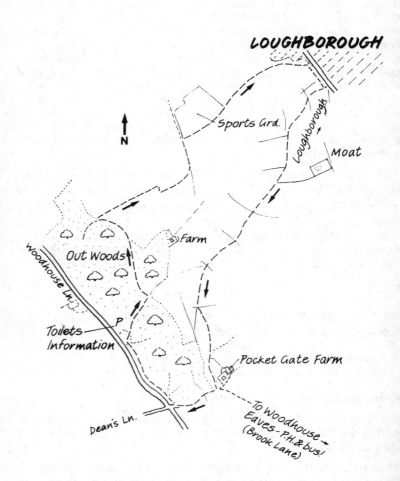

LOUGHBOROUGH

Sports Grd.

Loughborough

Moat

N

Farm

Out Woods

Woodhouse Ln.

Toilets
Information

P

Pocket Gate Farm

Dean's Ln.

To Woodhouse
Eaves – P.H. & bus!
(Brook Lane)

and Derby City Transport buses 121/122/123/124 go through Woodhouse Eaves. Ring Busline for details

Refreshment None on route. Nearest pubs and shops are in Woodhouse Eaves or Loughborough.

The route can be started at either end. It follows easy and ancient tracks between Loughborough and Charnwood. You do not need good weather to enjoy the walk!

Items of interest The Outwoods: a gift from the Moss family of Loughborough. Read the notice board for wildlife items to be seen.

Pocket Gate is an old way into Charnwood Forest from Loughborough. It was so well established as an ancient right of way that it was left as a hedged public route even when the area around it was made into a deer park in 1229. It is marked as a road on a map in 1762.

Moat House, once an important deerkeepers house. In the 18th and 19th centuries it became an elegant moated homestead, where John Oldershaw and Henry Whatton entertained on a lavish scale. We do not get a good view of the house, but the name on the map reminds us where the Deer Keeper lived when this was a deer park.

OUT TO THE OUTWOODS, THE POCKET GATE WAY
Loughborough   The Outwoods

1. **From the Outwoods car park** (Outwoods Cottage, Breakback Road, between Woodhouse Eaves and Nanpantan) note the toilets in the left corner and the wide track exit in the right corner. Take the wide track exit and make your way across the wood. Any of the permissive paths will do if you keep in the same general direction. The aim is to cross the narrowest parts of the wood, across the stream and hilly craggy ridge of rocks which form the spine of the Outwoods.

2. Meet the main track on the far boundary and turn left to walk with the wall on your right. Keep in this direction, passing impressive rocks on your left. The track bends sharp left by a seat and information board but we turn right to go towards Loughborough.

3. Go through the metal kissing gate and follow the well trodden path (K58) to Loughborough. The path is wired off and becomes a hedged path going gradually downhill on a gravelled track.

4. Meet a hedged lane from Outwoods Farm and turn left along it for a short distance.

5. At the sports field boundary turn right and keep close to the hedge on your left. It curves gently left beside the sports field and eventually meets the willow-lined stream in front of houses. Turn right. Keep the Woodbrook stream on your left to join the path which comes in from Moat Road and Valley Road on your left.

From Loughborough, Valley Road and Moat Road, follow the signposted Woodbrook bridleway (which leads from Queens Park to the Outwoods). From Valley Road it begins as a drive between gardens of houses.

6. Pass the little recreation ground swings and car park on your right and cross the cartbridge over the Woodbrook. Ahead lie the Outwoods, hilly and rocky. The 'devil's profile' rocks of Beacon Hill can be seen beyond them. Pass the end of the track to Moat House, and continue on the stony hedged track, going gradually uphill.

7. When the hedge on the left ends, keep on until you reach a spectacularly large isolated oak tree. Turn left and follow the track across the field, (parallel with the edge of the Outwoods). Pass a second large oak tree.

(To return to Woodhouse Eaves, if you started there, keep on this path to Pocket Gate and then follow the track past Hangingstone Farm into Brook Lane.)

8. To return to the Outwoods car park, turn right before you reach Pocket Gate and enter the Outwoods by the handgate and continue straight across the wood on the main path which leads to the Outwoods Cottage car park.

(To return to Loughborough if you started from there, turn right on the main path round the eastern edge of the wood and continue from paragraph 3.)

These most picturesque ruins are about 2 miles northwest from Newtown Linford. The scenery here having the two elements – wood and water – which are often wanting in so-called forest landscapes, is remarkably rich; and from a distance the grey towers of the ruin, rising above the ample foliage of its secluded, deep, romantic valley, render the scene very impressive.
Companion to Charnwood Forest 1858

Distance $5\frac{1}{2}$ miles ($2\frac{1}{2}$ hours on a brisk cold day. Much longer if you linger in the sunshine.)

Starting point Copt Oak.

How to get there Copt Oak is north of Markfield. From the A50 follow B587 signs to Copt Oak and Whitwick. From the A6 follow the B591 and B5350.

Bus routes There is a very occasional Bartons or Kinch bus (Route no 121) to Copt Oak. You would need to ask to be dropped off at Copt Oak. Ask Busline for details.

Refreshment The Copt Oak pub, not always welcoming to walkers.

The route Hilly. Poultney Wood is usually boggy and soggy underfoot at one point, but duckboards are provided. From Bawdon Lodge there are fine views. You can see the straight road going past Charley Chapel and, beyond the road, the little hollow of Alderman's Haw and above it, Beacon Hill. The modern windmills of West Beacon Farm can be seen turning very gracefully, just behind Charley Chapel.
Return by the same path from Ulverscroft Lodge Farm to Copt Oak. It is quite a climb up to Copt Oak.

Items of interest Poultney Wood, the lovely boggy area now managed by LRTNC (Leics and Rutland Trust for Nature Conservation).

Ulverscroft Priory, founded by Robert Bossu, second Earl of Leicester in 1134, for the Augustinian eremites. It was only a small foundation for a few inmates and it was dissolved in 1539 but during the time the monks farmed it a large area of the forest was cleared. The wild areas provided the monks with marvellous hunting and hawking grounds. The priory is now the finest monastic ruin in Leicestershire. The old prior's lodging is incorporated in the building.

Alderman Haws, once a monastery for a few monks.

Charley Chapel (Erected 1862) is now a private house. On the OS map it is not named, but marked with a small cross.

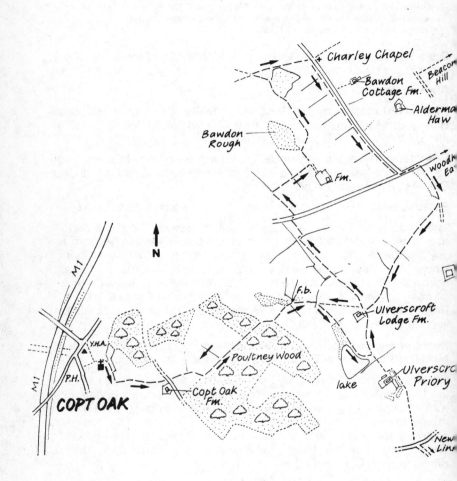

The ruined tower of Ulverscroft Priory founded by Robert Bossu, second Earl of Leicester, in 1134.

The romantic old buildings of the Prior's Lodge Ulverscroft.

Old English longhorned cattle near Ulverscroft Lodge farm. (The horns make the animals look more alarming than they are!)

THE HEART OF THE FOREST
Copt Oak   Poultney Wood   Ulverscroft

1. **From Copt Oak** pass the pub on your right and turn right at the footpath sign. Pass the church on your right and continue past the churchyard. Cross the stile and aim straight for the tall radio mast.

2. Turn left at the first mast and walk in a field with a second mast over to your right. Cross the stile ahead and walk with the wall now on your right. (The field has interesting ridge and furrow lines sloping down to the wood on the left. The farm ahead is Copt Oak farm.) Cross the fence to the left of the farm.

3. Cross the road (Whitcrofts Lane) to the footpath sign. Go over very awkward fences by the sheep pens and continue along the fenced-off track. Continue steeply downhill, with Ulverscroft Wood on your right for two fields, and beautiful views ahead. Go through the gate into the woods, still downhill on a good wide path.

4. Emerge from the wood and swing slightly right. Go through the gate and continue downhill, close to the hedge on your left. Cross the stile and footbridge and walk on the duck boards which keep you above the bog. Continue close to the stream on your left until you meet the footbridge which brings you out of the wood, Cross the concrete planks over the wet area of the far bank.

5. Turn right to follow the stream, keeping a little to the left of it. You are now heading for Ulverscroft Priory (Ulverscroft Lodge farmhouse stands very prettily up on the hill to your left.) Cross the waymarked stile and pass close to the lake on your right.

6. Meet the Ulverscroft Lodge farm drive and prepare to turn left. (If you want a closer look at the priory turn right here but return to this point to continue the walk.)

7. Walk along the drive towards Ulverscroft Lodge farm, with your back to the priory. Fork right to keep to the right of the farm buildings. Cross the waymarked fences and pass the farm on your left. (We shall be returning to this point later in the walk.) Keep the hedge and stream on your right.

8. At the far end of the next field move left to go through the gateway. Now go uphill in a long narrow field between hedges on your right and left. (If it is ploughed keep close to the hedge on your right.) The gap at

the top of the field leads onto a track which leads you close to the hedge on your right in the next field.

9. Meet the road and turn right for a few yards then left at the footpath sign (to keep in the same direction). Walk for one field, with Bawdon Castle farm sheds up on your right. Turn right and immediately left to cross the wall and walk uphill with it on your right. Cross the stile and follow the fence up to the farmsheds.

10. When you are level with the farm buildings turn left to follow the telegraph lines. (Some isolated clumps of bushes are all that remain of the lovely old walled track which once led to the farm.) By the telegraph pole, at the corner of the walled outcrop of rocks and trees, (Bawdon Rough) swing right and follow the curving (muddy) farmtrack, close to the wall on your right. Keep following the telegraph lines. The walled outcrop of Bawdon Rough is uphill on your left.

11. As you continue downhill, go under the telegraph lines and pass a pond on your left. Continue downhill for two fields, passing the wall of Cattens Rough, the field over to your right, with isolated stumps of rocks strewn around. The wall of Cattens Rough swings round away from you. (You can see it from the gate on your right in a corner of the field.) To reach it we have to continue downhill, keeping the hedge on our right. Halfway down the field look for a rough fence crossing on your right. This takes you into a field corner. Go diagonally uphill to reach the corner of Cattens Rough wall and continue in the same direction, over the hill and downhill to meet the road, at the field corner.

12. Turn right to pass Charley Chapel and continue along the pleasant road for half a mile. Over to your left there are lovely views of Beacon Hill (and windmills). Pass the drive to Alderman Haws.

13. Meet the B591 road and turn left for a short distance. Turn right, beside a wood, to walk along the drive to Black Hill Farm. At the end of the wood fork right to leave the farm drive and walk on a good headland, with the hedge on your left. At the end of the field join a wide tree-lined track to Ulverscroft Lodge farm. (The next field usually has interesting Old English longhorned cattle.)

14. Ulverscroft Lodge farm lies ahead. Cross the (awkwardly fenced) footplank beside the gate and turn right to pass the farm on your left. Move immediately left, uphill to cross awkward fences into a narrow fenced-off track. Go uphill through the spinney and pass the farmhouse over to your left. Continue in the same (diagonally right) direction to reach the far corner of the field. (Copt Oak Masts ahead seems very high above you!)

15. You now return to Copt Oak by the way you came. (A quick reminder for those who have forgotten:- cross the footbridge into Poultney Wood, near the bottom corner of the field. Walk with the stream on your right. Cross the duckboards. Walk uphill with the hedge on your right. Turn right and then left to go up through the woodland and go steeply uphill with the wall of the wood on your left. Make for the Copt Oak masts. Meet the fenced track which lead to the cattle pens/sheep pens. Cross the road near Copt Oak Farm. Walk with the field wall on your left. Cross the kink in the hedge. (Ignore the path to the left.) Keep close to the hedge on your right. At the mast turn right and pass through the churchyard. Turn left to pass the church and meet the road in Copt Oak.)

NINETY FEET SHORT OF A MOUNTAIN 16
Copt Oak   Bardon Hill   Old Rise Rocks

> Mr Sedgwick exclaimed, "The rocks are of igneous origin, and are entitled to be called mountains".
> Companion to Charnwood Forest 1858

Distance: 5 miles, with a possible short cut or extension.

Starting point Copt Oak. The village has a telephone box, twin radio masts, which are visible for miles, a pub, a church and a youth hostel, but no public facilities.

How to get there Copt Oak lies on the junction of the B587 from Markfield or Whitwick and B5350 from Loughborough and Stanton under Bardon.

Bus routes The 121 bus run by Barton Buses and Kinch Bus might be a possibility. Ask Busline for details.

Parking at Copt Oak needs tact and diplomacy. Parking is a problem as the roads are busy and the traffic fast on the B591. Only occasional buses to serve this small hamlet and there is no other suitable starting pont for this walk which takes you into the isolated heart of Charnwood. Copt Oak makes a marvellous walking centre. Some public parking space or a more frequent bus service would be a boon to walkers.

The Copt Oak Pub provides meals and has a big car park for patrons. It allows parking (for walkers who are customers) during the week but not at weekends or busy times.

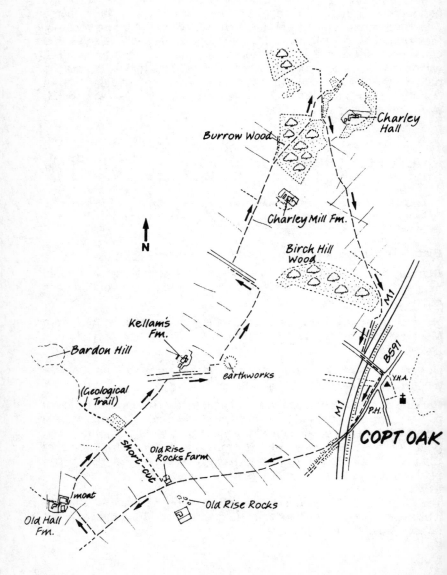

Charley Hall

Burrow Wood

N

Charley Mill Fm.

Birch Hill Wood

M1

Kellam's Fm.

Bardon Hill

earthworks

B591

(Geological Trail)

Y.H.A.

M1

P.H.

COPT OAK

Short-cut

Old Rise Rocks Farm

moat

Old Rise Rocks

Old Hall Fm.

There is parking space near the church for a few vehicles but the carpark is for use of churchgoers only.
The Youth Hostel has space but it is usually needed for hostellers.
The Memorial Hall has space. (Tel 01530 243 241 for permission.)
There are some grass verges

Refreshment The Copt Oak pub provides food and drink but is not really welcoming to walkers.

The route From Copt Oak you cross the Motorway and enter the true Charnwood forest, past Old Rise Rocks skirting the edge of what used to be medieval deer park, now destroyed by quarrying. Much of the route follows the old boundary of the former Whitwick deer park. The wall is visible near Rise Rocks farm. We follow the remains of the ditch and wall bank until we go down to Hall Farm.
There are steep climbs back from Charley and up to Bardon Hill (the optional extra). Otherwise easy.

Items of interest Bardon Hill is the highest hill in Leicestershire. At 912 feet above sea level it does not qualify as a mountain. It was once a beautiful deer park, surmounted by a summer house, chosen as a picnic spot for Queen Adelaide when she visited the county, but it is now only a shell, constantly eroded by quarrying. Its woods are mentioned in 13th century documents.
The climb to the summit of Bardon Hill is worth it for the view and for the spectacle of the vast quarrying operations in the heart of the volcano. It is signposted with the geological trail logo (a red diamond on a yellow base). The path once went right over the top of the hill and down to Agar Nook but quarry operations force us to turn back to the foot of the hill.

Copt Oak church is interesting as one of the three churches built after the Enclosure of Charnwood in 1808. The church, like the one in Woodhouse Eaves, was designed by Railton and built in 1837. Both are dark and solid with a simple granite tower.

Rise Rocks, (spelt Rice Rocks on old maps) three pyramidical points, with a boulder rock perched precariously on the lower slope.

Old Hall moated farmhouse is very attractively sited. The original farmhouse on this site was built in about 1450 and demolished in 1840. From here the route follows the ancient path which goes all the way to Kellams Farm and beyond into the heart of Charley. The large amount of holly in the hedges is an indication of ancient woodland.

Near Kellams Farm, we pass close to the raised low mound of a

The granite walled bridleway leading to Burrow Wood.

possible Iron Age settlement and the much higher mound of modern quarrying and dumping operations.

Birch Hill Wood is one of the oldest woods in Charnwood, named in 13th century documents.

Burrow Wood has many holly trees and large granite rocks. The wood is mentioned in 16th century documents.

The woods near Charley Hall are private but managed by LRTNC.

NINETY FEET SHORT OF A MOUNTAIN
Copt Oak   Bardon Hill   Old Rise Rocks

1. **From Copt Oak** pub pass the Youth Hostel and the telephone box on your right and turn left along the B591 towards Stanton-under-Bardon.

2. Cross the bridge over the M1 motorway. Fork right, down the embankment at the footpath sign. Cross the stile and swing left to cut across the corner of the first field to go through the gateway. Continue in the same direction across the next field and cross the waymarked double stile, which brings you out in the corner of a field. Walk close to the wall on your right for two fields.

3. At the end of the third field cross the drive to Old Rise Rocks farm and continue with the hedge, wall and farm-drive over to your right. Pass the outcrop of Rise Rocks on your left.

4. Pass the attractive Rise Rocks farmhouse, on your right. Go through the field corner. Here you meet a crossroads of paths. Our route goes straight on, to reach the moated Old Hall Farm.
The path to the right is a short cut to parag 8. It leads straight to Bardon Hill, going downhill parallel with the hedge on your right, across the slate bridge and then uphill close to the hedge on your right. The geological trail sign is just to the left of the top corner of the field by the wood.)

5. From Rise Rocks keep in the same direction, close to the hedge on your right for two fields. (The pretty tree topped hill over to your left is Billa Barra. A terrace of houses on the A50 road come into view ahead, but we turn right before we reach the road.)

6. Turn right in the corner of the second field and walk downhill, on the wide headland track, with the hedge on your right to reach Old Hall Farm beyond the bridge between two lakes of the dammed up stream. Stop to look at the water and to pat the ponies.

7. Ignore the path ahead and turn right to pass in front of the moated house and walled garden on your left and continue in this direction, close to the hedge on your left. Note on your right the short cut path which comes from Rise Rocks.

8. On your left look out for the waymarked geological route sign (a wigwam of red and yellow). You can follow it to go up to the top of Bardon Hill. It is an optional extra, well worth the effort. Return by the same route to this point.

9. From the foot of the hill, keep the hedge on your left and cross the fence by the gate. Continue in the same direction for two more fields. Meet the lovely tree-lined drive from Bardon Hall to Copt Oak.
The original line of our path went straight ahead, past Kellams Farm to meet the road, but quarrying operations have forced a diversion of the route. We now have to deviate from this original straight route and make our way round the most recent workings of Bardon quarry. This diverted route will be operational until the year 2000.

10. Turn right along the drive for 20 paces, passing Kellams Farm on your left. Turn left at the waymark sign by the drive to the farmbuildings but turn right immediately. (The waymark sign may be obstructed by old farm machinery.) Keep close to the hedge on your right, with deep ponds on your left. Follow the wired-off path and cross the high stepped stiles.

11. Now follow the pylons. The path moves diagonally left to cross the cartbridge. Continue diagonally across the next field and pass close to the low circular ditched mound on your right. (It is possibly the site of an Iron Age settlement.) Cross the stile and pass under the pylon in the corner of the next field.

12. Your next goal is the pylon in the top far left corner of the field but you need to follow the headland round two sides of the field. Walk uphill close to the hedge on your right and turn left at the top hedge. (This hedge is interesting because it was the boundary hedge and wall of the old deer park. The road runs beside it.) Continue through the little scrubby spinney and emerge in the open field with the new man-made hill ahead of you. Follow the hedge on your right and meet the drive from Kellams farm. You are now back on the ancient track.

13. Turn right and cross the road very carefully to reach the walled lane opposite, signposted as a bridleway for 600 yards. This leads you down past Charley Mill, very prettily sited with its lake and trees in a field on your right. Ignore the lane to the mill.

4. Continue straight ahead to the handgate a little further on (The bridleway ends where the lane curves left and we continue on the footpath.) Go through the handgate and walk downhill through the lovely Burrow wood on the path which leads to Charley Hall.

5. Exit from the wood through the handgate. The field ahead is interesting. It is a crossroad of ancient tracks. Note the gate over to your right, which leads to Charley Hall. The correct route for us to reach this gate is to go straight ahead, down the slope of the field, beside the remaining course of an old stone wall. Halfway down the field we need to turn right round and go back uphill, keeping close to a bank and deep gulley of a stream on our left.
The gate to Charley Hall is in the top left corner of the field.

6. From the gateway (usually muddy) ignore the sunken approach to Charley Hall ahead of you. Turn right. Keep in this direction, with the woods on your right.

7. Cross the waymarked fence and stride over the stone crossing where the stream makes a little cascade.

8. Turn right to cross the wall into the bottom corner of a big pasture field. You need to go diagonally up this field to the top left corner. (If there are any agressive looking horses, keep close to the hedge on your right or left and make your way round. I have walked the route many, many times, without trouble, but have received complaints, usually from people walking with dogs, who disturb horses. If in doubt, look for an escape route and report any difficulties to the farmer or the LCC Rights of Way officers at County Hall.)
It is quite a steep climb to the top corner

9. Keep aiming towards the left edge of Birch Hill Wood on the horizon ahead. Continue diagonally uphill. The next crossing is halfway along a wall under old telegraph lines. Go over the ladder stile. Keep diagonally left in the same direction to meet the wall of the lane from Charley Mill. (No waymarks here and poor crossings.) Cross the lane and continue diagonally uphill across the field to pass the corner of Birch Hill Wood.

10. Go through the gate in the corner of the field and continue close to the motorway down on your left, for two fields, with rather awkward stiles. Climb the flight of steps up to the road. Turn left and cross the motorway. Meet the B591 road. (The masts of Copt Oak sprout up behind the church tower ahead.).

11. To cross the B591 turn left to the traffic lights. At the far side of the road a little well-hidden path leads you through a metal kissing gate

and along a wooded path to Copt Oak church.

At Copt Oak church turn right along the drive to reach the pub on your left.

DRY-SHOD TO OLD WOODHOUSE
Quorn   Rabbits Bridge   Woodhouse Eaves

17

Directions to tourists:
'There is no publichouse at Woodhouse, but Woodhouse Eaves will afford stabling and refreshment for visitors to Pocket Gate, Beacon etc. None of the villages afford style, but in all of them stabling etc and comfortable accommodation are to be found.'
Companion to Charnwood Forest   1858

Distance 4 miles if you start from Quorn or Old Woodhouse and omit Woodhouse Eaves.
Add an extra 2 miles if you include Woodhouse Eaves

Starting points Woodhouse Eaves, Old Woodhouse or Quorn at the end of Meeting Street.

How to get there Quorn lies 2 miles south of Loughborough.
Old Woodhouse is just north of Woodhouse Eaves.
Woodhouse Eaves is signposted from Newtown Linford or Quorn.

Bus routes Woodhouse Eaves, Old Woodhouse and Quorn are all on regular bus routes.
In Quorn buses 125, 126, 127 (Loughborough to Leicester) stop near the Bulls Head, opposite Rawlins Community College.

Car Parking There is a big public car park with toilets in Quorn, near Wrights impressive old factory building by the crossroads of Meeting Street and Leicester Road. You will need to walk along Meeting Street to join the walk. (There is limited roadside parking in Meeting Street.)
The car park in Woodhouse Eaves is on the main street near the big Methodist chapel.
There is only street parking in Old Woodhouse.

Refreshment Several pubs at Woodhouse Eaves and at Quorn. No facilities at Old Woodhouse.

The route A very easy walk, mainly on tracks. One section of track, near the old railway line is called Dirty Lane! Take note!
The fields are mainly pasture or arable fields with good headlands. The stiles are good.

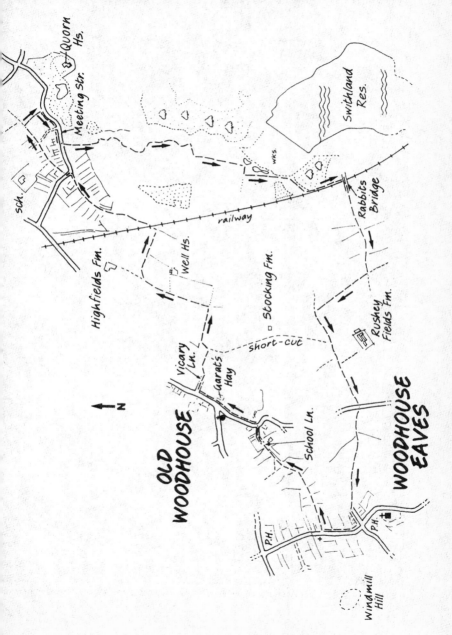

Pestilence Cottage, Old Woodhouse, where Thomas Rawlins came after escaping from the plague in 1665.

Items of interest In Quorn the walk starts from Meeting Street, a road full of interesting old houses. The old baptist chapel is dated 1770.

The path between Woodhouse Eaves and Old Woodhouse is well surfaced – a reminder that this path would have been the "Sunday Best" route for churchgoers from Woodhouse Eaves who attended Old Woodhouse church before their own was built.

Pestilence Cottage, Old Woodhouse, where Thomas Rawlins came after escaping from the Plague in London after his father died of the pestilence in 1665.

In Old Woodhouse there are pretty cottages which Mrs Perry Herrick built for her tenants. The front doors are so arranged that the women could not easily stand on their doorsteps to chatter to one another!

Swithland reservoir is only a few hundred yards off our way, and well worth the detour.

Buddon Hill once an ancient settlement but now completely destroyed and scarred by quarrying. (Quernstones were quarried here.)

DRY-SHOD TO OLD WOODHOUSE
Quorn   Rabbits Bridge   Woodhouse Eaves

1. **From Quorn** follow Meeting Street until you reach the footpath sign opposite no 21. Go through the wide gateway which leads to Quorndon Mill. Leave the drive when it swings left. Continue straight ahead and walk beside the meandering stream on your left.

2. Meet the wire fence on your right and cross the stile in the corner of the field. Turn left to continue in the same direction with the hedge on your left. At the end of the field, where dark trees block your way, a footbridge leads you across the stream and sharp right, beside the railings of the beautifully landscaped, but very private, water gardens of the Severn-Trent Water Authority.

3. Cross the footbridge into an open field, and move right to meet the railway line in the far corner. Walk beside the railway in the next field. Meet the lane by the railway bridge (Rabbits Bridge).

4. Here you turn right, but to see the lovely Swithland reservoir with its impressive viaduct turn left for a short distance along the lane and then return to the railway bridge to watch for steam trains tooting by.

5. Cross the railway bridge and continue along the lane. Pass Rushall Field Farm, the first farmhouse, on your left and turn right at the next footpath sign. Go downhill close to the hedge on your right then turn left

A view into the opulent Victorian water treatment grounds of Swithland Reservior, opened in 189

(to pass the tall farm silos of Rushey Fields Farm uphill over to your left).

6. Short cut return **to Old Woodhouse**, from Rushey Fields Farm, omitting Woodhouse Eaves: Meet the concrete drive which comes down from the farm and turn right to go through the waymarked gate. This wide concrete drive takes you uphill past the big house of Stocking Farm and along to a junction where the drive bends left into Vicary Lane, Old Woodhouse or goes on towards Well House (paragraph 9).

7. To continue **to Woodhouse Eaves** cross the concrete drive and keep close to the hedge on your right until you meet the road. Cross carefully and continue in the same direction. Pass the school on your right and walk up Meadow Lane to the crossroads. There are two pubs opposite and a bus stop to your right. Woodhouse Eaves recreation ground carpark is along the road to your right.

8. **From Woodhouse Eaves** leave the recreation ground carpark, opposite the imposing red brick Methodist Chapel, follow the tarmac strip past the sports field, keeping close to the wall and hedge on your left until you reach the Water Board railings. Cross the stile on your left and cut across the corner of the field to where the hedge juts out. Here you join the stream on your right, through a tree-lined path, into School Lane, at Lane End Cottage. At the road, turn left to Old Woodhouse church, passing Pestilence Cottage on your left, and continue through the village.

9. **From Old Woodhouse** turn right at Vicary Lane and walk along the tarmac drive. Turn left at the junction, signposted to Well House, and follow the path as it swings right. At the end of the first field the path bends left, when it meets the 'Private Road' sign. You are now walking towards the flat Loughborough plain. The carillon tower is visible in front of you.

10. When the drive bends right, to Well House, go straight on across the field towards Highfields Farm. Before you reach the house, turn right to join a hedge. Walk with this hedge on your right towards Buddon Wood, Mountsorrel quarry and the Great Central railway line.

11. Turn left under the railway bridge and follow the green lane which moves gradually away from the railway. When the lane opens up, swing left to cut across the corner of the field to join the unadopted road which leads into Chaveney Road. Follow Chaveny Road into Meeting Street, Quorn.

1293 King Edward I granted John Comyn, Earl of Buchan, a market (at Whitwick) on Tuesdays and a fair on the eve and day of St John the Baptist and two days following.

1306 Elizabeth, widow of Alex Comyn, earl of Buchan, crowned Robert the Bruce King at Scone and was by command of Edward I set on the walls of Berwick Castle in an iron cage (while her son Alexander, Earl of Fife was at his manor of Whitwick).

Nicholls, History and Antiquities p 1112

Distance 5½ miles. (Short cut, omitting Swannington, reduces this by a mile.)

Starting points Thringstone or Whitwick or Swannington

How to get there Whitwick lies North-east of Leicester, 2 miles north of Coalville. Follow the A50 and turn off via Copt Oak on the B587 .
Thringstone is 2 miles further along the road. From Loughborough it can be reached from the A512.
Swannington is 2 miles from Coalville, on the A447 which links the A512 and the A50.

Bus routes and car parking.

Whitwick is on a regular bus route. Ring Busline for details. There are bus stops and a public car park in Vicarage Road at the foot of Leicester Road, opposite the City of Dan with its big mining wheel monument.
Thringstone has bus stops and public car parking on the Green near the Rose and Crown.
Swannington is on a regular bus route from Ashby de la Zouch. There is no public car parking but the pubs providing food might allow parking for customers.

Refreshment

Whitwick has innumerable pubs and a fish and chip shop
Thringstone has several pubs and Ruby's Fish Shop on the Green.
Swannington: The Fountain Inn serves food. The Post Office sells snacks, drinks and confectionery.

The route: Very varied. Hills and rocks, small stretches of quiet road, heath and pasture land. The walk through Cademan Woods (mainly silver birch and oak) is lovely. There are very impressive old boulders beside the path.
The short cut omits the main street of Swannington by walking along Red Hill Lane to meet the Swannington Incline.
The way into Whitwick is along the Country Park path past the lake at Whitwick Leisure Centre and along the old railway line into Whitwick.

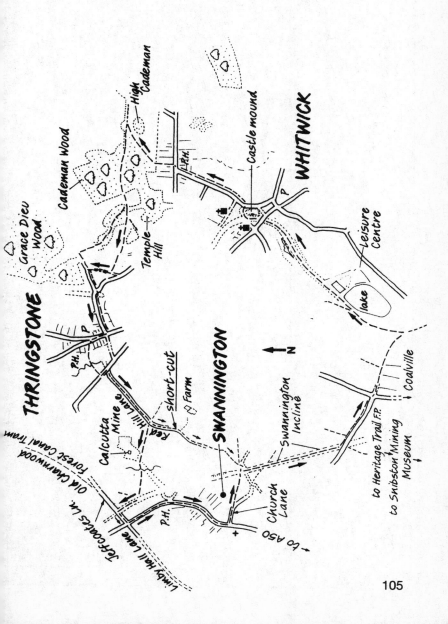

The rocky tor of High Cademan with Cademan and Grace Dieu Woods.

Items of interest

Whitwick has 2 churches, an old nunnery, several chapels, a castle mound, an impressive leisure centre and a recently established walkway along a disused railway line. The little ticket office of the old station is now Whitwick History group HQ. The steps at the back lead down to the railway line now a walkway. (Public toilets and church are a little further along the road to Thringstone.)

Swannington is described as a 'place where cole is gotten' in a King John charter of 1205. William Wyggeston was lord of the manor here in 1520. The turnpike road from Hinckley to Melbourne came through the remarkably long village street in 1760.

In 1779 a horse drawn tramway was planned to take coal from the nearby pits to connect with the canal wharf at Thringstone Bridge. When this failed a railway was built in 1833 for the cheaper transportation of coal from Swannington directly to Leicester and Loughborough. The line, built by the Stephensons (George and his son, Robert) ran from 1833 – 1870. This was the first use of steam locomotives in the Midlands. It necessitated the construction of an Incline and a powerful stationary winding engine at the top to help trains up the gradient of 1 in 17. A rope was used in the centre pulleys as a safety device for runaway trains on this steep climb.

The Swannington Incline is now cleared as part of the Heritage Trail. The notice boards make interesting reading.

High Cademan, an impressive outcrop of rock in Cademan woods. If you are sure you can get back to the point where you leave the track, it is well worth the detour to climb it. But do not attempt to do so unless you have time to loiter and good strong footwear. The descent can be quite steep and it is easy to lose your way.

New permissive paths are planned through the woods and the old Stations of the Cross route over Broad Hill, Twenty Steps and Calvary may soon be open to the public (Dec 1996). Look out for waymark signs after you have crossed Cademan Moor.

COALS TO CHARNWOOD
Whitwick   Thringstone   Swannington

From Whitwick:

From the car park near The Three Horse Shoes pub (City of Dan), go up Chapel Street to meet the main road. (Buses stop here.) Turn right along Market Place and North Street to reach the parish church. Cross the railway line bridge. Pass toilets on your right.

1. Turn right at the footpath sign by the grey towered church. Follow the tarmac drive through the churchyard passing the church on your left. (Note the spout of clear water emerging from churchyard.) Pass the dismantled old railway track which comes in from your right.

2. Pass Whitwick Castle Hill mound which rises up on your right. Join the little lane past houses on The Hockley.

3. Meet Cademan Street by the Castle Garage and turn left. (The Roman Catholic redbrick church and the interesting old convent in dark granite are on your left along Parsonwood Hill. A small detour to see them also gives you fine views down over Whitwick and over to Temple Hill and Cademan woods, our next goal, over to the right.)

4. At the top of Cademan Road turn right and prepare to turn left just before the Man Within A Compass inn.

5. Turn left at the footpath sign between houses 121 and 127 (!) A stile at the end leads into the pub garden. Walk close to the wall on your left and cross the stile at the end of the garden. This leads you into Cademan Woods.

6. Through Cademan Woods the main track is waymarked but the signs are a bit vulnerable. You need to go slightly right, with your back to the wall and keep firmly in this direction until you meet the far wall boundary of the wood. So take note of the direction and ignore minor tracks! Go steeply uphill past rocks and go over the rocky ridge. The huge rock of High Cademan is on your right.

7. Cross one main path and continue on a smaller path going slightly downhill to reach the wall ahead. Turn left here (but stand to admire the wide open view to the north before you turn west to follow the wall on your right).

8. Keep straight on in the same direction on the main track (still following the remains of an old wall, but ignoring the outer wall which turns away to the right).

9. At the edge of the wood, cross the fence in the walls ahead and emerge in the open field of Cademan Moor. Continue straight across the field, parallel with Temple Woods over to your left, with extensive views to your right of Breedon, Osgathorpe, Belton and points north.

10. Go over the fence in the wall gap to enter a second belt of woodland. Two paths fork here. The one on the right goes uphill and over the rocky outcrops of Broad Hill, Twenty Steps and Calvary and to meet the Turolough Road, with Thringstone down to your left. The one on the left goes downhill, passing large rocks on either side.

11. Near the end of the wood, fork right to cross a little gap in the wall and continue towards a big white house beyond the wood. Cross the stile and follow the wired-off path which leads past Turry Log Farm (a much extended house). Cross the drive and continue downhill to the road. Note Carr Hill rock on your left and a single huge rock in the field on your right. There are lovely views. Ahead are Coleorton church spire and Coleorton Hall, big and white on the horizon. Emerge at the footpath sign on Carr Hill Road. Turn right to pass Turry Log House and meet the Turolough Road.

12. Turn left and go downhill into Thringstone.
Thringstone Green is on your right.

From Thringstone leave The Green by the footpath at the side of the Rose and Crown pub.

13. Pass the Rose and Crown pub on your right and follow the wide drive between high granite walls. Go through the little spinney, cross the stile and go steeply downhill close to the hedge on your right, to cross the good concrete bridge over the stream. Continue uphill to the stile by the footpath sign onto the road.

14. Turn left along Talbot Lane (a main road from Peggs Green) for a few yards and then go right, up Red Hill Lane.

15. Red Hill Lane leads to the top of the Swannington Incline. (If you use it as your short cut to omit Swannington, cross the road bridge when you reach the Incline and descend the steps. Continue from parag 20.)

From Red Hill Lane to Swannington: at the top of the hill turn right at the footpath sign and go downhill parallel with a hedge on your left. The tall winding gear of the old Calcutta mine and pumping house stands below in the valley. Cross the waymarked stile just to the left of the building. As you go downhill note that you are aiming for Coleorton Hall and the old windmill base ahead.

16. Cross waymarked stiles in little pasture fields and go over the track leading to the mine building. (It is the dismantled tramway track between the Calcutta mine and the Swannington Incline.) Turn left to walk with the tramtrack bank on your left and cross the substantial handrailed footbridge over the stream. Continue with the stream on your left and make for the stile on your right in the narrow end of the field.

17. Two paths meet here. Turn left to join the Swannington railway line and then turn right to walk along it.

18. At the road junction turn left (Jeffcoates Lane) to the cross roads with Limby Hall Lane. Turn left on the long main village street of

Swannington. Pass the Fountain Inn on your right and the Post Office on your left. (It is a long stretch but interesting for its variety of old buildings, big houses set up high on the right, little terrace cottages set below the present street level.)

19. At Church Lane turn left (past the old Quaker house on the corner) and go downhill past the entrance to Manor House. Keep straight on when the lane bends right. Follow the well walked path across the field to the top corner. Cross the stile onto the Swannington Incline.

20. Turn right and walk up the Swannington Incline track, passing under the new road bridge of Red Hill Lane and the high wooden footbridge which carries the old Potato Lane track over you. At the top of the Incline pass the foundations of the old engine house and follow the line of railway track to meet the road. (The Mining Heritage trail continues on the opposite side of the road and leads to Snibston mining museum and Discovery Park. Leave that for another day.)

21. Turn left at Spring Lane. (This is a busy road but there is a pavement and the views over to the hills of Charnwood are very fine.)

22. At the junction with the main B585 Coalville-New Swannington road, cross carefully and continue in the same direction along the green lane bridleway (a welcome alternative to the busy noisy main road). Go downhill on the good track. Whitwick RC church is over to your left. Ignore the first footpath (to New Swannington) on your left but take the next one. Cross the golf course. Move gradually to the stream over to your left.

23. Keep close to the stream on your left. Pass the lake on your right. (Ignore the footpath over the footbridge on your left. It is a pleasant path to the cemetery on Church Lane Whitwick, but we can follow the old railway line into Whitwick.)

24. Pass the leisure complex on your right and keep on the clear track until you pass under the railway bridge (with the steps up to the old ticket office on your left). Whitwick parish church is on your left and Castle Mound on your right.

THE LONG LOST CHARNWOOD FOREST CANAL   **19**
Thringstone   Grace Dieu   Osgathorpe

> Charnwood Forest Canal . . . its bed remains a memento of abortive speculation. But although it somewhat impedes agriculture, it is a rich field to the botanist.
> Companion to Charnwood Forest   1858

Distance   4½ miles

Starting points Thringstone or Osgathorpe.
In Thringstone there is a public car park on the green, the junction of Loughborough Road and Main Street. No public parking places in Osgathorpe.

How to get there Thringstone lies on the B587 a mile NW of Whitwick, just north of Coalville and west of Loughborough and Shepshed.

Bus routes Regular buses between Coalville and Loughborough pass through Thringstone. More frequent buses between Whitwick and Thringstone. Details from Busline.
No bus service to Osgathorpe.

Refreshment Thringstone has several pubs but there is no food at Osgathorpe (The Royal Oak Pub doesn't serve food, but B and B is available.) Better take a picnic.

The route Very varied. There is a choice of old main roads with interesting buildings in Thringstone or more modern housing estate roads of Swallowdale, where little jitty walkways take you parallel with the stream and the woods. The Swallowdale route is less architecturally interesting but it is the quieter, the gardens are attractive and you do meet pleasant people, including many retired and rehoused miners. You can make your own choice. When you reach the recreation ground and football pitch in Swallowdale, turn right.

A lovely woodland stretch takes you to Grace Dieu manor (now a prep. school), followed by a quarter of a mile of busy road, with the prettiest verge possible. Walk along a country road towards Belton, a lane into Osgathorpe and a treelined footpath along the old Forest Canal back to Thringstone where there used to be a wharf tramway connection for coal transport.

Items of interest Thringstone has interesting old buildings and lots of jitty footpaths on both sides of the road.

Grace Dieu priory ruins. The priory was founded for Augustinian nuns in 1242. Roesia de Verdon the heiress to the estate paid a sum of

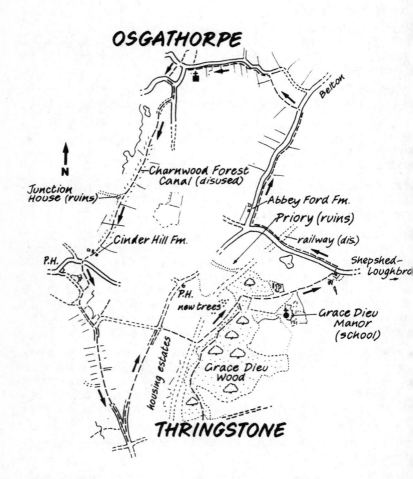

money to the king to enable her to remain single after her father and husband died. She invested her money in the foundation of the nunnery in 1239 and was buried there in 1247.

In 1306 John Comyn (of Whitwick castle) granted one hundred acres of land to the nunnery. After the Dissolution of the Monasteries the disposal of the nunnery lands was 'surrounded by avarice and sharp practice'. The house was closed in 1538, on the 30th of March of the 30th year of the reign of Henry VIII (1509–1547). Sir Humphrey Foster acquired the land but soon sold to the Beaumonts, who retained it until 1683, when it was bought by Sir Ambrose Phillipps of Garendon.

Grace Dieu Manor stands in the grounds of the Augustinian priory. The house was designed by William Railton and altered by Pugin. Charles Booth once lived here. His wife was a founder of the Women's Guild, which became the WI.
The house is now a prep school for boys and girls, boarding or day pupils.

The Charnwood Forest Canal was planned in 1790 to speed the transport of coal from Swannington and Coleorton to Loughborough, where it could travel by the River Soar (canalised since 1778) into Leicester. It was constructed to follow the 300 ft contour line to avoid the costs of locks and the route makes big loopy meanders which must have been very pretty but very time consuming. There were tramway connections at each end with rails to carry loads uphill from Swannington to the canal wharf at Thringstone and down again from Nanpantan to Loughborough. A feeder reservoir for the canal was constructed at Blackbrook and completed in 1796 but burst in 1799 and was dismantled in 1804.

The Charnwood Forest Railway Line was constructed in 1882, utilising much of the canal route. The railway was able to take a more direct route, avoiding some of the canal loops and bends, because trains could tackle slight changes in contour. The line was closed by 1963 and abandoned by 1965. Parts are now public footpaths.

Osgathorpe is a tiny hamlet, named in Domesday Book. The tiny church has parts built in 1204. Osgathorpe school and almshouses 1670–80. Interesting old houses include a rectory and the Tudor timber framed Manor Farm. The new road just to the north doesn't impinge on its quiet charm. The Royal Oak pub does not serve food (though you might like to check this. Pubs do change their services.)

Grace Dieu Woods. It may soon be possible to walk through the woods on permissive paths. If the permissive routes are opened you will be able to make a beautiful start to this walk instead of following

113

Loughborough Road or the Swallowdale streets. It is worth walking from Thringstone up Grace Dieu Road and along Turolough Road to see if the permissive path is open and waymarked. if it is you can walk through the loveliest of woods to follow the stream. Meet the drive which comes down from Grace Dieu school. Turn left to cross the old bridge over the stream and join the route at parag 4.

THE LONG LOST CHARNWOOD FOREST CANAL
Thringstone   Grace Dieu   Osgathorpe

1. **From Thringstone** walk towards Loughborough. Follow the main road until you reach the sign opposite Henson Lane.

2. Turn right to reach the recreation field. Pass the football pitch and in the far corner of the field, turn left. The stream and Grace Dieu woods are now on your right and a new plantation of Forestry Commission trees (part of the new National Forest) on your left. Continue close to Grace Dieu woods on your right.

3. At the end of the field enter the lovely old woods of Grace Dieu. A waymarked path takes you across the main track which comes over a wide stone bridge on your right.

4. Cross this track and keep in the same direction to follow the little path over the concrete plank bridge. Turn right (the stream bends away from you) and continue into the open parkland field with Grace Dieu school in its lovely setting ahead of you.

5. Walk close to the hedge and the ponds in the old rocks on your left. Pass close to Manor Farm. When you are level with Grace Dieu school cross through the (awkward) fence in the narrow wall gap and follow the lovely wide conifer-lined drive to the road. Belton church lies ahead.

6. Turn left at the main A512 road. Pass the mounds of the old railway bridge. The ruins of Grace Dieu nunnery are in the field on your left. The Grace Dieu Parish boundary stone indicates Loughborough 7 miles and Burton on Trent 14.

7. Turn right to follow the Grace Dieu Lane towards Belton and Osgathorpe. Fork right on the road signposted to Belton 1½ miles. Pass Abbey Ford farm. There are fine views of low hills, little woods, pasture fields and Belton church spire ahead. A footpath comes in on your right from the Grace Dieu brook and crosses the road.

8. Turn left at the footpath sign and walk close to the hedge on your right until you meet the lane into Osgathorpe

9. Turn left and walk along the pretty road beside the white-railed stream towards the little spire-capped tower of Osgathorpe church. The route of the old Charnwood Forest canal can be just about detected at the top of the narrow fields on your left by the 30 mph sign near Cottage Farm buildings

From Osgathorpe we turn left after passing the church but it is pretty to cross Dawsons Bridge and then turn left to walk beside the stream .

10. Turn left at the road and and follow Snarrows Road from its junction with Chapel Lane

11. Near the top of Snarrows Lane we take the footpath on the right. Our route is now generally south, following the bed of the old canal. The canal banks are hardly visible at first. Keep close to the hedge on the right. (The definitive map says right of the hedge but the stile is on the left of it.) In the second field the path becomes a very obvious bed of canal and high towpath bank.

12. Pass the remains of Junction House, where the canal forked. Keep in the same direction. Cinder Hill Farm lies ahead. The path goes between the house and the farm buildings. It is not waymarked. You are supposed to walk with hedge on your right at first (though the old canal is clearly visible on other side) and then turn right to enter the farm yard. (This needs clear waymarking and improved stiles fixed by the gates.)

13. Join the drive from Cinder Hill Farm house and meet the road.

14. A little waymarked path on the opposite side of the road enables you to cut off a corner of busy road. Cross the stile and the farm drive and go over the stile on your left. Pass the farm sheds to reach a third stile (into the field with a donkey). Turn left and then right to reach the far corner of the field, where you meet Lily Bank Lane, Thringstone.

15. Fork left to reach Thringstone main street.

IN SEARCH OF AN EXTINCT VOLCANO
Whitwick   Mount St Bernard's
Blackbrook Reservoir

> **The guest master informs me that in hard winters he has known poor people to come from towns and villages six or eight miles off, to obtain here what they could not obtain elsewhere – a plentiful meal.**
> Charles Dickens, Household Words, on Mt St Bernard's Abbey
> quoted in Companion to Charnwood Forest   1858

Distance 5 miles

Starting points Whitwick or Mt St Bernard's Abbey. Mt St Bernards Abbey has no public transport but it does have a big car park, a little tourist shop, open at certain times only, and toilets.

How to get there Whitwick is north of Coalville and can be reached from Copt Oak on the B587.
For Mt St Bernard's Abbey turn off the B587 or the A512 and follow signs for Oaks in Charnwood. The abbey is between Oaks in Charnwood and Whitwick.

Bus routes. 117 buses run approximately hourly from Leicester to Whitwick. Ring Busline for details.

Refreshment At Whitwick and at The White Horse pub, Shepshed, at the half way point.

The route 6½ miles (This could be cut to 5 miles by starting at Mt St Bernard's Abbey and omitting Whitwick by walking along a mile and a half length of very pleasant road.) Magnificent views in this hilly and rocky volcanic area around High Sharpley.

Items of interest
Mt St Bernards Abbey : The first Roman Catholic monastery built in England since The Reformation. The foundation stone was laid in 1843. (The Catholic Emancipation Act was passed in 1829.) Ambrose Phillipps de Lisle, born in 1809 was converted to Catholicism when he was 16, bought land in Charnwood and gave it to the Cistercian Order. A small group of monks cleared the ground and built the chapel (designed by Wm Railton) in 1837. In 1840 the Earl of Shrewsbury, of Alton Towers, gave money for the abbey (designed by A W Pugin).

A hoard of Roman coins and weapons were found near the site of the abbey.

Blackbrook Reservoir, a beautiful little reservoir in a setting of pinkish volcanic rocks. You can loiter on the bridge and watch the water birds which feed there. An earth dam for a reservoir was built here in 1792 to

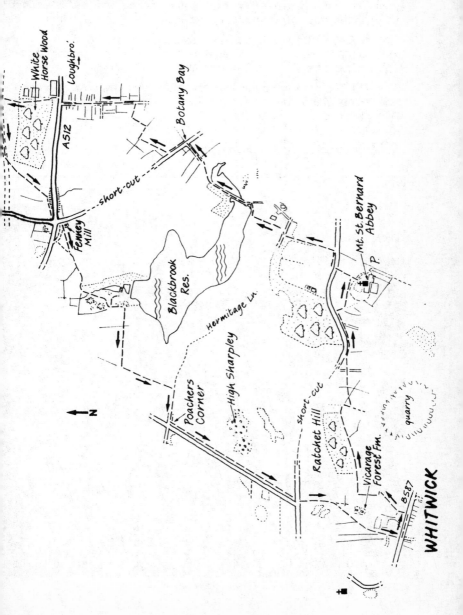

feed the Charnwood Forest Canal but a rapid thaw after a heavy snowfall caused it to collapse in Feb 1799. The present structure dates from 1904/6. In 1957 there was an earth tremor which caused much water to escape but since then many school parties have gone through the inspection tunnel and returned safely to tell of its marvels.

Botany Bay Cottages. The name was quite popular for houses in the 19th century, when the first penal settlement was set up for convicts shipped out to Botany Bay in Australia.

The Old Charnwood Forest Railway. The short stretch of dismantled railway built partly on the route of the Charnwood forest canal is now designated as a public path,
Paradise, the site of an old isolation hospital.

Fenny Windmill is now a private house.

Blackbrook Reservoir and the high point of Ives Head.

Peldar Tor quarry can be seen after you have passed Ratchett Hill and before you reach Mt St.Bernard's Abbey. The track round the quarry affords spectacular views down to the quarry pool, where the accumulated volcanic deposits are now being blasted for roadstone.

The site of the original volcano which erupted in the High Sharpley area was long thought to be in Peldar Tor. It is now believed to have been in the heart of Bardon Hill.

IN SEARCH OF AN EXTINCT VOLCANO
Whitwick   Mount St Bernard's   Blackbrook Reservoir

1. **From Mt St Bernard's Abbey** go to the main road and turn right for 100 yards towards Oaks in Charnwood. A footpath sign on the left takes you downhill through woodland, close to a wall on your right.

2. Cross Hermitage Lane and continue downhill with a hedge on your right. One Barrow Lodge is over to your right.

3. At the bottom of the field turn right and cross a rough pasture. Turn left along the drive which comes from One Barrow Lodge. Cross the bridge over the Blackbrook reservoir and continue to the main road.

4. Turn left at the road junction, passing Botany Bay cottage on your left. Walk towards Fenney Mill (*a possible short cut to paragraph 10, if you need one) and pass one field on your right.

5. Turn right at the footpath sign. Walk close to the hedge on your right to join a barbed wired track which takes you to the right of a big house. Turn right to meet Brick Kiln Lane. Turn left down Brick Kiln Lane to meet the main A512 Ashby to Loughborough road. (The White Horse pub is just to your left along the road.)

6. Cross the A512 road and turn right for a short distance to the footpath sign. Turn left, down to White Horse Wood.

7. The path passes just inside White Horse wood, beside a chain link fence on your right. Cross the footbridge in the small stretch of open ground and turn left along the dismantled railway footpath.

8. Just before the railway bridge, where the houses end, turn left to pass White Horse wood. (The correct route is to descend right and swing left, under the railway bridge.) From the bottom corner of the field, with White Horse wood uphill on your left, you need to move diagonally away from the wood, over the brow of the hill and down to the far corner of the field.

Gun Hill House nestling in the rocks of the forbidden High Sharpley.

9. Turn right into 'Paradise field' and cross the stile onto the little track which goes up a steep bank to Tickow Lane crossroads.

10. Turn left to cross the busy A512 road, towards Fenney windmill, going along the Charley Road for a few yards. Take the little lane on your right and cross the stile near the water board building. Cut across the corner of the field and go through the stone squeeze-through stile to rejoin the lane.

11. Follow the lane towards the lovely landscaped grounds of Blackbrook reservoir water works. When the lane swings left, continue straight ahead up the walled track. Go through the handgate into an undulating open field.

12. Turn left and go uphill close to the reservoir wall on your left. Turn right in the next field and walk with the hedge on your right. At the end of the field do not got straight on towards the road but turn left to continue with the hedge on your right. Meet Hermitage Lane and turn right to Poachers Corner.

13. **From Poachers Corner to Whitwick** (1 mile) turn left along Swanimote Road to pass Cademan wood on your right. At the bottom of the hill turn left along Oaks Road (short cut to Mt St Bernards) and immediately right along the drive to Vicarage Forest Farm. After 200 yards turn right at the footpath sign and make your way across the field to the right of Vicarage Forest farmhouse, where the wall makes an angle. Follow the wall and hedge all the way down into Whitwick, crossing Hogarth road and emerging at no. 77 Leicester Road.

14. The centre of Whitwick lies to the right. The route to Mt St Bernard's goes left.

From Whitwick to Mt St Bernard's Abbey go up the Leicester Road. Turn left along the track (opposite number 120) past the quarry bank. Pass a small playing field on your left and keep on up the track, which swings right, near Tower House. Ratchett Hill wood is on your left and the newly planted quarry slope on your right.

15. Meet the track which leads up to the quarry and turn right. We turn left at the stile and aim for Mt St Bernard's abbey (but it is worth the slight extra distance to continue to the quarry edge to see into the depths of the hole and return to this point).

16. From the lane to the quarry cross the stile and continue in the direction of Mt St Bernard's, going diagonally over four fields. Meet the road and turn right.

17. Turn right at the footpath sign and go up to the abbey through a

belt of trees. Turn left at the top of the path and walk with the abbey grounds on your right until you reach the main drive to the abbey.

Turn right to the carpark.

A GEOLOGICAL TRAIL
Whitwick   Warren Hills   Holly Hayes   **21**

Whitwick is situate on the border of Charnwood Forest in a sharp and cold situation, having several high hills and rocks on the north side: yet the inhabitants are in general healthy.
Nicholls, History nd Antiquities p 1112

Distance 5 miles (plus optional short extension to Mt St Bernard's Abbey)

Starting points Whitwick carpark at the foot of Leicester Road/ Vicarage Lane, opposite the City of Dan.
Mt St Bernard's Abbey if you want a slightly longer walk.

How to get there Whitwick is just north of Coalville. From the A50 from Leicester fork off on the B587 through Copt Oak. Pass the Bulls Head and continue down to Whitwick.

Bus routes Bus 117 runs approximately every hour and stops near Whitwick church. Ring Busline for up-to-date details.

Refreshment The Bulls Head on the A50 road near the Warren Hills makes a good break. It is 787 feet above sea level, the highest pub in Leicestershire, and a very welcoming place to eat and drink.
Or picnic on the Warren Hills.
There are many pubs in Whitwick, but I have never found a good eating place there yet. Tea and (minimal) snacks are available at the Hermitage Leisure Centre.

The route permissive paths through lovely old woodland, with wide variety of plants and birds, a short stretch of road uphill, gentle walking along nature reserve land with geological trail of interesting volcanic rocks, an optional extension along the farm drive to Mt St Bernard's and back down to Whitwick. An amazing variety in such a short walk. If you want a longer route, add on walk 20, from Mt St Bernard's when you reach paragraph 10.

Items of interest
Whitwick Holy Cross RC church, with its tall redbrick tower, was built in 1904. The Crapper Almshouses opposite were built 1846.

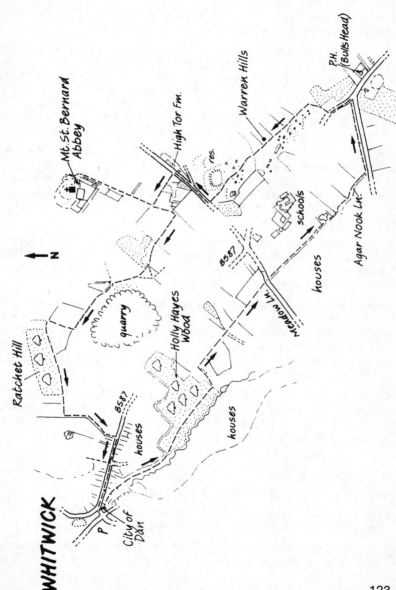

The Parish Church dates back to the 13th century but it has been restored in more recent times.
The castle mound is close to the church.

Hermitage Sports and Leisure Centre has a swimming pool and provides drinks and snacks.

Holly Hayes wood is an ancient woodland, coppiced since1600. The paths through it have recently been opened to the public as permissive paths (courtesy of ARC quarrying and North West Leicestershire County Council). It is now a favourite leisure spot for local people. Walkers prefer the paths through the wood to the definitive paths where the houses have encroached on the edges of the wood. Woodpeckers and jays can be seen as well as less colourful birds.

Mt St Bernard's Abbey. Ambrose Lisle March Phillipps de Lisle, who converted to Roman Catholicism when he was 16, founded the monastery in 1835 for Cistercian monks. The Earl of Shrewsbury funded the building and the church was designed by Pugin and begun in 1843 and enlarged in 1934. The stalls were designed by Eric Gill in 1938.

The old reformatory was the original settlement for the few monks who built with their own labour the original dwellings. It was later used as a reformatory for young offenders (mainly from Liverpool) who proved too much of a handful for the monks.

Warren Hills Nature Reserve and Geological Trail. From the top of the hill you have extensive views over the great flat valley with Hugglescote and Ravenstone down to the south west and Ratchett Hill and the quarry to the north west, with, on a clear day, Breedon Hill church beyond. The majestic tower of Mt St Bernard's Abbey comes into view to the north.

Peldar Tor quarry. It is possible to look right down to the quarrying operations below. There is a viewing platform and a fenced path where you can look down into the deep volcanic hole, with its tiered roads and its lorries like toy cars. Huge rocks line the path.

A GEOLOGICAL TRAIL
Whitwick   Warren Hills   Holly Hayes

From Whitwick start from the little public car park at the foot of the Leicester Road, at the junction with Vicarage Lane.

1. Cross the road to the City of Dan, with its mining wheel monument on the green. Follow the tarmac strip over the footbridge. Pass a Grace

Dieu Valley Project notice board. We now follow permissive paths. Cross the footbridge and go between grassy slopes and the brook on your left.

2. Cross a second bridge and keep on the well walked path with the stream on your right and houses of Holly Hayes Road over to the left. Holly Hayes Road turns left into Birch Avenue but we go straight on to the dead end of the road and go through a gap in the row of huge boulders, by a notice board of items to be seen in the wood. Keep in the same direction, close to the pretty stream on your right At the end of the wood meet a little weir and pond with ducks and other water birds.

3. Turn left, passing the notice which gives quarry blasting times and follow the wide track towards the huge ARC shed, with the wood now on your left. Pass the huge commemorative rock (the explanatory plaque has been vandalised).

4. Turn right along the main path (the 022, with fine views of Warren Hills and rocks of Peldar Tor to your left, and Bardon Hill mast ahead of you) and follow it to the road (Meadow Lane).

5. Cross Meadow Lane and keep in the same direction on a footpath which goes beside the school playing fields and the backs of house gardens. (This path should by law be wide enough for two people to pass or to walk side by side. As it is narrow many people trespass along the school field edge.) Cross the access road to the primary school and continue on the lane to meet the main road from Agar Nook

6. Turn left and walk uphill on the long straight road from Agar Nook (There is a pavement and very good views.) Meet the main A50 Copt Oak-Whitwick Road. The Bulls Head pub is 150 paces to your right and well worth the detour! To reach it you pass Abbot's Oak with its lovely gardens, on your right.

7. Walk along the main road towards Whitwick. Pass one house on your left and turn right at the footpath sign into the nature reserve of Warren Hills Go uphill on the well walked path across one open field. Go through a gap in the wall, then swing left onto the Warren Hills.

8. You now have the choice of following the lower wall, along the waymarked geological trail or going up to the top wall and following the footpath over the hills. Or do both! Begin by following the waymarked geological trail, which follows the wall on your left and gives marvellous close up views of fantastic rocks. When you meet the wall corner, turn right and walk up the hill to meet the footpath, turning left to follow the high ground, along the ridge.

9. Meet Abbey Road at the footpath sign and turn right. Go downhill to

High Tor farm and turn left through the metal handgate by the lodge house (dated 1856) on the drive to Mt St Bernards Abbey. (Note the walls on the left, where the old reformatory stood.)

10. At the bend in the path decide whether you wish to make the short extension to visit the abbey. If you do, continue along the drive and return to this point after your visit.

To return to this point **from Mt St Bernard's Abbey,** pass to the left of the toilets and the farm buildings and follow the wide farm lane to the bend in the lane, where you turn right to follow the waymarked geological trail.

11. From the bend in the lane go through the wide gateway and turn left uphill on the waymarked geological trail. Pass close to a house on your left. Cross the stile and turn right to walk along the fenced-off path close to a wall on your right. Pass outcrops of rocks in the field on your left and the abbey over to your right. Continue to the field corner and cross the stile into a scrubby area with gorse.

12. At the wall end turn right, passing close to a huge rock on your right. Cross the concrete wall-stile and take the right hand fork in the path, keeping close to the wall on your right. When the wall ends swing right on a main track. Steps lead up to a viewing point to the quarry and the track swings right on a wide track by pine trees.

13. The footpath is signposted down to your right. It crosses a little walled enclosure and then swings left to keep close to the quarry bank and field edge. (But for an even more extensive view of the quarried rocks, you can continue on the gravel track on the high ground beside the quarry, and then descend the steep gravel track to rejoin the footpath, which meets this track.)

14. Both routes follow the wide drive down from the quarry towards the Oaks Road and High Sharpley rocks. The chimneys of Gun Hill House can be seen set in the rocks ahead.

15. Half way along the drive, turn sharp left and walk uphill between Ratchet Hill on your right and the smooth rounded slopes of the re-seeded Spring Hill on your left. The path goes gradually downhill between newly planted trees and the ancient rocks of Ratchet Hills enclosed in the lovely silver birch wood on your right. Pass Tower House over to your right. The track bends left and continues downhill to pass the flattened area of an old sports feld.

16. Meet the wide gravel drive which leads to the Leicester Road, opposite number 120. Turn right and walk downhill to the centre of Whitwick.

Postscript: save our rocks from the quarryman's blast.

BIBLIOGRAPHY

There are too many authorities to list. Hoskins and Pevsner and Nicholls go without saying, for reference, as do Arthur Mee's The King's England and JB Firth's Highways and Byways in Leicester. I find myself constantly referring to the WI Village Book for Leicestershire and Rutland (and wish that more little villages had WI groups!)
For readable geology I am indebted to: AE Trueman: Geology and Scenery in England and Wales (Penguin 1961, 1st pub. 1938) and the very handy LCC leaflet Geological Walks in Charnwood Forest (An excellent little publication! Cheap enough to buy and small enough to carry with you!)

A few books I am particularly indebted to are:
Charnwood Forest, A Changing Landscape (Loughborough Naturalists Club) 1981
The Medieval Parks of Charnwood Forest (A E Squires and W Humphrey) 1986
Charnwood Forest (CN Hadfield) 1952
Joan Stevenson's various books on Charnwood and Bradgate Park and lots of local leaflets from libraries, information centres and village stores on my travels.
Bardon Hill: A Source Book: Concerning the Ancient Enclosure of Bardon Park (Len Noble)

OTHER LOCAL WALKING GUIDES FROM CORDEE

THE CHARNWOOD ROUND   Heather MacDermid
A map guide to the 33 mile circuit of Charnwood Forest. A challenge walk with a difference; to be taken as one long walk or divided into four easy stages, by using the short cuts fully described.
ISBN 1 871890 12 8   £2.95

FOXTON LOCKS TO RUTLAND WATER   Heather MacDermid
This guide takes you on the author's favourite walks through the beautiful but less well known countryside of East Leicestershire. You can choose the length of walk that suits you best. A short walk of 4 or 5 miles stopping to explore as you go along: or add on another circuit to make a long figure of eight if you like, and perhaps another to make it a clover leaf of eight or twelve miles. ISBN 1 871890 05 5   £4.95

THE ROBIN HOOD WALKS   Nottingham Wayfarers'
From the mediaeval gatehouse of Nottingham Castle to the ancient oaks of Sherwood Forest, the 105 mile long Robin Hood Way takes a meandering route, linking many hisorical sites with some of the major tourist attractions north of the River Trent. 14 circular walks based on parts of the Robin Hood Way are also included as medium-length family walks. ISBN 1 871890 02 0   £4.95

60 NOTTINGHAMSHIRE WALKS
Nottinghamshire Ramblers' Association
Varied walks from every corner of the county suitable for all, compiled by members of the Nottinghamshire Ramblers' Association to celebrate the 60th anniversary of The Ramblers' Association, plus a bonus of 5 heritage walks in the city and surrounding towns.
ISBN 1 871890 77 2   £6.95

All CORDEE books are generally available at most bookshops and outdoor recreation shops in the area. They are also available at local libraries and Information centres. If they are out of stock ask them to order these from Cordee, 3a De Montfort Street, Leicester LE1 7HD. If you wish to order direct please add 10% for postage and send us your cheque.

Please ask us for a copy of our comprehensive 32 page stocklist of outdoor recreation and travel books/maps from the world's specialist publishers.